RESPONSIBILITY *in* BUSINESS

decisions, issues and ethics: a case-study approach

Val Winch & Roy Watson

Hodder & Stoughton

LONDON SYDNEY AUCKLAND

British Library Cataloguing in Publication Data

Winch, Val
    Responsibility in Business: Decisions,
    Issues and Ethics – A Case-study
    Approach
    I. Title   II. Watson, Roy
    658.4

    ISBN 0-340-56732-5

First published 1992

Typeset by Wearset, Boldon, Tyne and Wear.
Printed in Great Britain for the educational publishing division of Hodder & Stoughton Ltd, Mill Road, Dunton Green, Sevenoaks, Kent by Thomson Litho Ltd.

Contents

Acknowledgements

We would welcome further correspondence on the issues raised.

Acknowledgements are gratefully made to the following: Ethical Consumer magazine who have provided us with more than a source of inspiration; Tony Ward, Bristol Mediation who helped in the initial stages, providing much material and inspiration; Tony Weekes, for his correspondence, his time and advice; Liz Weir at Constantine and Weir for help in preparing the profile of Cosmetics to Go; Bob Lowman at the Ecology Building Society for help in preparing the profile of EBS; our colleagues at Bournemouth and Poole College of Further Education, Bob Baker, Rob Garner, Caralyn Longhurst, Jim Pope, and Marion Strongman, for their suggestions and support; Joanna Scudamore, for some typing and source material; Steevie and Sam Watson for their inspiration and encouragement; all the organisations who talked to us and gave us information; and to everyone who has ever caused us to stop and consider the results of our actions.

The authors and publishers would also like to thank the following for permission to reproduce material in this volume:

Cadbury Ltd for the photograph on p. 13; Ark for the photograph on p. 15; Ecoscene for the photograph on p. 16; National Power PLC for the photograph on p. 23; Green Ark Ltd for the logo on p. 23; J Allan Cash Photolibrary for the photograph on p. 24; Constantine and Weir PLC for the photograph on p. 26 and for the material on pp. 30 and 32; Options/IPC Magazines for the photograph on p. 31; Levi Strauss and Co.; Friends Provident and The Homeowners Friendly Society for the extracts from their brochures on p. 14; Harvard Business Review for the extracted material on pp. 11–12.

Foreword

The materials in this in-tray case-study are designed to provide students with an introduction to ethics in a business setting.

The case-study is particularly recommended for use with students taking the following courses:

BTEC National (Diploma and Certificate) Business and Finance
Common Skills and Working in Organisations
C & G 361 level 3 Communications skills
NVQ level 3 Secretarial and Administration courses
Supervisory and short management courses

Other courses, such as some GCE A levels, and GCSE courses, where communication skills, problem solving and group interaction are required components will also find it useful.

Students are given a scenario, organisation chart, and set of documents to be sorted and acted upon. These provide the opportunity for research and discussion upon the issues, and for practising the skills of organisation, time management, communications and group co-operation.

The materials relate to the following topic areas:
Personnel
Health and Safety
Equal Opportunities
Advertising, PR, marketing
Environmental issues
Human rights

The case-study is designed for flexible use, either on a regular basis over a series of lessons, or as an individual component of a business studies course according to the time available. It is designed to be open-ended so that students work at the appropriate level. Many of the documents interrelate and have implications for each other.

Suggested strategies for using the materials are included in the Introduction for lecturers.

Courses for which this book is recommended

The case study offers scope for developing communication skills, as defined in the specifications of several courses.

Additionally, it broadens the scope, challenging students to think for themselves on topical issues, and to reassess some of the traditional attitudes embodied in such courses.

By using the case-study, students are able to achieve objectives and demonstrate competences required by the following bodies:

1 BTEC National Certificate and Diploma in
Finance
Tourism
Public Administration
Distribution

Aims of the BTEC National Qualifications

- To develop vocational skills, knowledge and understanding which enable learners to be competent and immediately effective in employment in organisations in the public and private sectors.
- To assist learners to be flexible in response to the changing demands of business and society.
- To enhance learners' motivation and provide the opportunity for the development of personal qualities relevant to supervisory and management work.
- To promote in learners a positive and dynamic approach towards working in business and the public sector.

The Core Modules: Working in Organisations specify outcomes which can be achieved through use of the case study. It may be appropriately used with reference to Core Modules 1.3, 1.4, 2.2, 3.1, 3.4, 3.5, 4.2, 4.3, 6.1, 6.2, 6.3, 7.2, 8.1, 8.2, 8.3, 8.4.

Common skills
The Common Skills, to be included in all Core Modules, include 18 competences. By involving the students in team work, decision making, problem solving and considering the opinions of others, the case-study provides opportunities for most of these competences to be demonstrated.

Competence 1 Manage own roles and responsibilities
Competence 2 Manage own time in achieving objectives
Competence 3 Undertakes personal and career development
Competence 4 Transfer skills gained to new and changing situations and contexts
Competence 5 Treat others' values, beliefs and opinions with respect

Competence 6 Relate to and interact effectively with individuals and groups
Competence 7 Work effectively as a member of a team
Competence 8 Receive and respond to a variety of information
Competence 9 Present information in a variety of visual forms
Competence 10 Communicate in writing
Competence 11 Participate in oral and non-verbal communication
Competence 12 Use information sources
Competence 13 Deal with a combination of routine and non-routine tasks
Competence 14 Identify and solve routine and non-routine problems
Competence 15 Apply numerical skills and techniques
Competence 16 Use a range of technological equipment and systems
Competence 17 Apply a range of skills and techniques to develop a variety of ideas in the creation of new/modified products, services or situations
Competence 18 Use a range of thought processes

2   City and Guilds 361 Levels 2 and 3

The case-study covers the following Objectives:

a   Receive and interpret information in written and graphical forms
b   Communicate effectively in written and graphical forms
c   Communicate effectively in oral form

In particular, students are given the opportunity to work on areas where traditionally 361 material has been limited.

3   GCE Advanced and Advanced (supplementary) General Studies

The aims and objectives of this subject, set down by several examination boards, are satisfied by the case study.

AEB states that the aims of the course are for students: '. . . to develop a broader outlook and demonstrate their interest in and commitment to contemporary issues.'

Assessment objectives include:

3   Evaluate and interpret contemporary issues in an interdisciplinary context
4   Organise and present material in an appropriate and coherent form
5   Carry out independent research involving initiative, determination and the ability to draw conclusions

The case-study is relevant to topic themes 1, 2, 3, 5 and 6.

London University's Advanced Level Objectives include:

1 To use a variety of communications skills, numerical, verbal and literate
2 To think objectively, even in areas where problems of value judgement seem paramount
3 To use interpretively skills 1 and 2 above, particularly to make reasoned *connections* between different aspects of a topic, and to *transfer* such thinking to the world they live in.

Advanced Supplementary Level positively encourages 'open' teaching techniques.

The case-study covers objectives:
1 Language skills
4 Appreciation of current trends and developments in society.

4 GCE Advanced Level Law

AEB includes in its assessment objectives:

2 Ability to analyse factual problem situations and apply appropriate substantive legal rules and principles.
4 Ability to appreciate the effects of law and the legal system upon the individual and society.

5 Other business, secretarial and management courses

The materials can be used with students of different ability levels and work experience backgrounds. Therefore, some of the documents in the case-study, if not all, will provide stimulus material for students on a variety of courses. The student-centred learning method is advocated by many examining bodies, and certainly this problem solving approach has proved popular with our students.

Other courses on which the case study materials could be useful include short courses on:

business studies
management skills
business ethics
personnel aspects

More advanced secretarial courses which contain elements of management appreciation and personnel functions include:

LCCI   Private Secretary's Certificate
LCCI   Private and Executive Secretary's Diploma
RSA   Higher Diploma in Administrative and Secretarial Procedures

Students on these courses would find some of the case-study materials appropriate.

To assist lecturers in identifying suitable materials, all documents are numbered and listed under topic headings.

INTRODUCTION
FOR STUDENTS

What does 'ethics' mean?

What do you think it means to say that someone acts ethically? Perhaps you think it means that someone follows particular rules of behaviour, but what rules? Where do they come from? Here are some attempts to explain what 'ethics' means.

- Ethics deals with the values of human life.
- Ethics is concerned with the type of conduct or character that is approved of or disapproved of in terms of right and wrong or good and bad.
- Ethics is concerned with the principles that guide people in making choices in their daily lives.

Think about these statements and try to draw up your own definition of ethics and to explain what it means to act ethically.

The structure and purpose of this book

When you enter the world of business you will find that you are often confronted with problems which have an ethical dimension. The aims of this book are to prepare you to deal with such problems and to encourage you to think about issues of right and wrong. The authors have prepared an extended case-study of a fictional soft drinks manufacturer, Harwoods. The case-study is structured around a collection of memos which might be found in the in-tray of any supervisor or manager. You will be asked to read the memos and undertake a range of activities relating to them. The memos are grouped around seven themes:

- personnel
- ethical investment and ethical consumerism
- Health and Safety
- Equal Opportunities
- advertising, PR, marketing
- environmental issues
- human rights

It is important to remember that these themes are not isolated; most of the problems covered interconnect with each other. You should try and spot the connections wherever possible.

The meaning of words

Whilst working through the in-tray exercises, you will need to think very carefully about the meaning of words. In daily life we sometimes unduly restrict our use of words, for example, 'cost' may be seen exclusively in financial terms, but there are costs other than financial costs. Read through the following list of key words and think about the questions accompanying each one. These are the sorts of questions you might ask yourself when working through the in-tray exercises.

- Cost: is the only type of cost financial? Can we talk of the ecological cost of a business? How do we balance different types of costs against each other? Which is greater, the cost of having or not having catalytic converters in a fleet of company cars?
- Value: is 'value' a monetary term? Do we value intangibles like quality of life? Do we value the wellbeing of others and how high a priority can we give this? How can a business add value to a community?
- Price: does 'price' only mean what you pay for something? What price do we pay for a society based on mass production, convenience shopping and private transport by car?
- Success: how do we measure success? Can we talk about a business being ethically successful?

Ethics in business

Businesses have power through their ability to spend large amounts of money. They have the ability to enhance or change situations that the individual does not. As they affect many people, they have obligations to their employees, to the consumer, to the community, and perhaps to the whole world itself. They have a responsibility to act, not only in a way which is not harmful, but in a way which positively benefits all these, as well as themselves. However, this is not straightforward, as conflicts of interest are inherent between these groups. Decisions therefore need to be taken with an informed awareness of these conflicts and according to some system of principles.

Codes of conduct

Many businesses have created what they have called codes of conduct or ethics codes; these are lists of what they believe to be ethical behaviour. However, the existence of a code may not guarantee ethical conduct from the company. The codes have often been drawn up in response to scandals and to protect the name of the company, merely stating its legal responsibilities and the conduct it expects from its employees rather than listing any ethical principles and aspirations that it holds. The emphasis has often been on the company setting standards for employees to meet so it will not be caught breaking the law, rather than on realising that the company itself needs to be guided in its business conduct. However, some companies have attempted to operate in a different, more global manner, for example, Levi Strauss.

Levi Strauss and Co.

Levi Strauss and Co. as a company is very visible. Its products are everywhere. Levi's has always had a good reputation for commercial success, concern for its workforce, and for social values. In 1987 it produced an 'Aspirations Statement' defining the values that the management and workforce shared. The result is an innovative and flexible company. Levi's has allowed itself to be led by a group of managers from traditionally disadvantaged sectors of the population in the creation of an equal opportunities facet to its Aspirations Statement. This excerpt outlines more fully what the company wants for itself and its employees:

> 'We all want a company that our people are proud of and committed to, where all the employees have an opportunity to contribute, learn, grow, and advance on merit, not politics or background. We want our people to feel respected, treated fairly, listened to, and involved.'

Levi's has asked, 'What kind of leadership is necessary to make our Aspirations reality?' In its answers it has borne in mind the following aspects.

- New behaviours: Levi's is looking for leadership that exemplifies directness, openness to influence, commitment to the success of others and willingness to acknowledge the leader's contribution to problems.

- Diversity: the company is looking for leaders who value a diverse workforce with respect to age, sex and ethnic group and who are committed to taking full advantage of the rich backgrounds and abilities of all staff. Leaders must seek differing points of view and reward, not suppress, honesty.

- Ethical management: leaders must try to epitomise stated standards of ethical behaviour.

The Statement also discusses recognition, communications and worker empowerment, and is a genuine attempt to change some of the more autocratic strategies of the past and replace them with a shared set of values and goals. The statement shows that the company has taken responsibility for its actions and is attempting to change these.

Judging a company to be ethical

Whether or not a company has an ethics code, it can be assessed against a number of criteria and its ethical position can thus be determined. Criteria used in assessing a company's ethical position could include the following.

- Environmental: what is the company's attitude to recycling, pollution and the greenhouse effect?

- Worker's rights: does the company respect its employees' right to belong to a union? Is there a constructive dialogue with the workforce?

- Human rights: does the company trade with countries with a poor human rights record?

- Women's rights: what is the company's policy on maternity rights and childcare facilities?

- Equal Opportunities: does the company pay men and women equally?

Does it have a scheme to monitor the number of people it recruits from traditionally disadvantaged sections of the population, e.g. women, ethnic minorities. Are its premises accessible to the disabled?

- Exploitation of developing countries: does the company exploit developing countries, e.g. by marketing inappropriate or harmful products to them?

- Animal rights: does the company respect animal rights and avoid inflicting suffering on animals?

You might like to try to identify examples of such organisations.

Other factors which might be taken into account include the managers' attitudes to pay incentives (do they award themselves higher pay increases than they do the workers?), automation and new technology (will they risk making people redundant by introducing automation?), and Health and Safety issues (are workers asked to work unacceptably long hours and put at risk of injury in order to meet orders?).

The criteria mentioned above are not the only ones. If you were trying to decide whether a possible employer was an ethically sound employer, which criteria would you use when making your judgement? Why would you use these criteria?

Ethical investment

John Cadbury 1801–89: a famous Friend

'The guiding principle which a Friend should keep in mind in making an income, whether by work or by investment, should be to the good of others and of the community at large and not simply of himself (sic) and his family. He should even at the risk of loss, strive to be strictly honest and truthful in his dealings: he should refuse to manufacture or deal in commodities which are hurtful to society and should be on his guard against obtaining an undue profit at the cost to the community. If he is an investor he should think not only of security and the rate of interest, but of the conditions under which his income is produced and the effect which investment in a particular field may have on the welfare of his fellow men, whether at home or in the less well developed countries of the world.'

This is from the Quaker handbook *Christian Faith and Practice,* and is a good place to start when considering ethical investment.

Ethical investment trusts give an investor the chance to invest his or her money in a way that meets with his or her principles, and not to invest in ways that go against these principles. For example, an ethical investment trust might invest a client's money in a publishing company striving to provide cheap books for students in the developing world, but not in a cosmetics company which exploits animals in its product testing, or in a company developing high-tech aids for the disabled, but not in a car manufacturer. Can you think of some similar examples? If you had some money in an ethical investment trust, how would you want it to be invested?

Typical statements of the aims of an ethical trust are made in these excerpts from company brochures:

'We avoid companies involved in polluting the atmosphere with dangerous gases, dumping toxic waste at sea or contributing to the erosion of the ozone layer by producing harmful chemicals.'

'Investments are also directed away from companies involved in the arms trade, experiments on animals or businesses actively contributing to health hazards and countries with oppressive regimes or dictatorships.' (Friends Provident Stewardship Fund)

'Green Chip backs companies that really do care about protecting nature, improving the workplace, and providing a cleaner, brighter world to live in. It offers you high growth potential without exploiting our environment, and with the security of Homeowners' expertise behind you.' (Homeowners Friendly Society Green Chip Investment Fund)

Ethical investment is the fastest investment growth area of the 1990s. In the USA, socially responsible investment is worth over $100 billion. In Britain, the Stewardship fund, initiated by Friends Provident in the mid 1980s, is now worth well over £150 million and the Ecology Building Society, which only gives mortgages to preserve and restore existing buildings, is the most rapidly expanding building society in the country.

Of the more mainstream financial concerns, the TSB and Co-op banks have both introduced ethical investment schemes.

Ethical consumerism

Have you ever stopped yourself from buying a product because of ethical considerations, or bought a product, such as environmentally-friendly washing-up liquid, because its use accords with your principles?

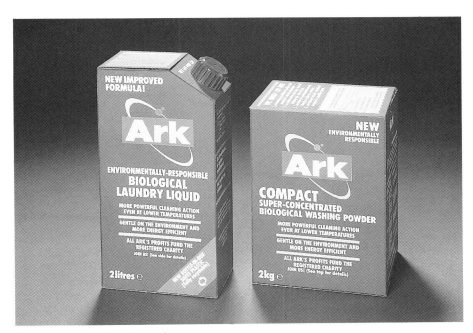

Environmentally-friendly products

Simultaneously in the UK and the USA, the idea is emerging that consumers, businesses and investors, by exercising their buying power in an ethical manner, can become a force for positive change in society. When consumers realise that they can create the products they want, the economic process will have to take account of their significance.

There are many consumer groups. One well-known American campaigner is Ralph Nader. See if you can find any information on him.

Ethical consumerism is about using your spending power to create the world that you want; a classic example is the boycott of South African goods which may well have contributed to recent changes in that country. Others include the introduction of health foods and vegetarian foods into mainstream supermarkets, more widespread recycling facilities, and the increasing use of non-rainforest woods in furniture making.

These have all come about as a result of the recognition that people want a different style of product. The motivation was not from product design committees but from consumers themselves, and manufacturers had to respond.

Today, bottle banks are in use all around the country

Decision-making questionnaire

You will soon be moving on to the in-tray exercises. When working through the memos you will be forced to make a number of decisions. The following questionnaire was designed to help management analyse their decisions. It may help you in your decision-making about the cases which follow.

	Yes	No
1. Does my decision treat me, or my company, as an exception to a convention that I expect others to respect?	☐	☐
2. Would I repel customers by telling them of my decision?	☐	☐
3. Would I repel qualified job applicants by telling them of my decision?	☐	☐

4. Have I been cliquish? ☐ ☐
   If 'Yes' answer 4a–4c
   If 'No' go to 5

   4a. Does my decision unfairly discriminate against a ☐ ☐
       particular group?
   4b. Does it divide the company? ☐ ☐
   4c. Will I have to pull rank to enforce my decision? ☐ ☐

5. Would I prefer to avoid the consequences of this ☐ ☐
   decision?

6. Did I avoid any of the questions by telling myself that ☐ ☐
   I could get away with it?

(Hyman, Skipper, Tansey)

If you have answered 'no' to all these questions then you have *probably* made the right decision!

A few final questions

When you are working through the rest of this book, you might like to think about the following (difficult) questions. There are no right or wrong answers to these questions, but thinking about them should help you with the in-tray exercises.

- Are right and wrong subjective? Can people ever agree about what is ethical?
- The end justifies the means – is this an ethical statement?
- Is non-action the same as acceptance? If we do not do anything about a situation, are we sanctioning it?
- Why should we be good?
- Are there consequences of unethical business practice – socially? psychologically? physically?

INTRODUCTION

FOR LECTURERS

- What are the conflicts and complexities of acting responsibly in workplace situations?
- Why do companies choose to abide by or to ignore ethical considerations?
- What is the relationship between a company's legal responsibility and its moral responsibility?

This book may assist lecturers who share the authors' belief that the discussion of questions such as these should be central to a student's business education. Students need to be aware of the ethical dimensions of business because ethics is integral, not marginal, to successful business practice. In order to promote debate on important issues the authors have developed an extended case-study based around the activities of a fictional soft drinks manufacturer, Harwoods. The case-study is built up out of a series of memos relating to difficult moral questions. The memos are similar to those which might be found in any manager's in-tray. Students may be asked to undertake a range of activities in connection with the memos. Some suggestions for activities will be given in a moment. They are suggestions only; the authors do not want to be prescriptive and have designed the material to be flexible.

The case-study can be used with students of widely differing abilities taking almost any general studies or business-related course. Lecturers may choose to teach only one or two hours of ethics, or to structure a whole term's work around the case-study.

By working through the case-study, students will be able to practise a wide range of transferable skills. Amongst other things, they will be encouraged to:

- develop written and oral communication skills in a variety of contexts;
- increase their awareness of the needs and motives of people at work;
- evaluate and interpret contemporary issues in an interdisciplinary context;
- organise and present material in a coherent form;
- think objectively even in areas where problems of value seem paramount;
- make reasoned connections between different aspects of a topic;
- treat others' values, beliefs and opinions with respect;

- gain an insight into the administration procedures used in large firms;
- relate to and interact effectively with individuals and groups.

Suggested strategies for using the case-study

Lecturers might find the following lesson plans useful. They are suggestions only, and not prescriptive.

Organising and prioritising

Divide the class into groups of four or five. Ask each group to organise the tasks which arise from the documents in order of priority for action; perhaps set a deadline to make the task realistic. Students should not only give suggestions for immediate action, but also consider long-term policy changes. A spokesperson should be elected to present the group's conclusions to the class. Once all the groups have reported back, general discussion can take place on the decisions made. Students should examine the criteria they have used for making decisions; these might include company image, legal responsibilities, staff welfare, cost, importance of the issue to society, and likely coverage in local media.

Introduction to a single theme

Divide the class into groups of four or five. Each group should select a theme, e.g. personnel, and members should read through all the memos relating to that theme. Within the groups, students should then discuss the issues raised and suggest possible solutions to the problems. A spokesperson should summarise the group's discussion for the class and perhaps a written report could be prepared. Again, once all the groups have reported back, there could be a general discussion. Later, individual students might undertake further tasks and go on to:

- research current news items relating to the theme and collect a file of cuttings;
- research the legal aspects of the issues raised and prepare a presentation on relevant legislation;
- take one aspect of the theme and research it in depth.

Follow-up activities

i) Elect student observers to watch their colleagues during group decision-making processes and report back on group dynamics. Observations could be made under a range of headings, e.g. ability to develop ideas, ability to justify ideas, willingness to listen to others, encouraging others to express ideas, co-operation, etc.

ii) Elect a panel of students to act as the Harwoods managers and ask the rest of the class to persuade them to accept a particular decision or adopt a particular policy. This exercise, designed to develop skill in presenting a coherent argument, can be built around a single memo or a group of memos relating to a theme.

iii) Individually, each student should write a report for Mr Horowitz, analysing the situation presented in a given memo. The report should summarise the problem, identify the principles involved and reason cogently for a particular course of action, making a reference to current events and using other supporting evidence where appropriate.

iv) Individually, students should write all the necessary communications, letters, memos, notices, notes for the personnel file, etc., which might arise from discussion of a given memo within Harwoods.

v) Assign roles to students and use the memos as a basis for role-play activities. As well as encouraging communication skills, role-play lends itself to the use of video which may be used to help students analyse their self-presentation.

Interrelation

The items in the in-tray are grouped around seven broad themes:

- personnel
- ethical investment and ethical consumerism
- Health and Safety
- Equal Opportunities
- advertising, PR, marketing
- environmental issues
- human rights

This grouping, although convenient, is somewhat artificial. Many of the cases are interrelated, reflecting the complexity of business activities and of the ethical issues themselves. Some topics, such as the rights of women and the role of unions, are discussed under broader headings. Wherever possible, students should be helped to spot the connections between different issues.

ETHICAL BUSINESSES: TWO PROFILES

The following profiles are of ethical businesses. This does not mean that the businesses involved believe that they are ethically perfect, but that they try to operate around stated principles, which take into account factors other than the need to make money, and that they are constantly trying to improve their operations in order to live up to their own expectations.

Why don't you write to a business of your choice and ask whether it is an ethical business, comparing the reply with the profiles below?

The Ecology Building Society

What is an ethical investment? In broad terms, ethical investment means being sure that your money is not causing ecological, moral or environmental harm. More positively, it means putting your money where you are assured that it will do some good.

Most of us considering such an investment will need to know that the vehicle for our savings will avoid supporting issues that we ourselves would avoid. For example, does the fund invest in countries where there are oppressive regimes? Are companies which are known as major polluters part of the investment portfolio of the fund where our money is placed? Are the investment managers positively discriminating in favour of socially conscious schemes or projects which promote energy saving? We must ask questions if we want to be sure of the ethical use of our money.

Can a building society be a place to make an ethical investment? Societies do not fall into the same category as the growing number of green funds being offered by insurance companies and banks. These are usually based on unit trusts where the investors' money is spread through a range of companies and projects. The value of units can rise or fall and any gain is normally taken over a long term. An ethical green fund of this nature has a portfolio according to the emphasis required by the fund managers. Building societies are different. Starting their lives as mutual, self-help clubs over 200 years ago, they have grown into familiar sights in the high street with well-known names reflecting the towns of their origin, e.g. Halifax. Specialist societies, such as the Temperance Society, have either changed their names or been swallowed up in mergers, losing their identity. The Ecology Building Society is one of the few remaining specialist societies.

The basic function of a building society is to assist people to purchase a home of their own. It invites investment and savings from individuals or groups to provide a fund for this purpose. Investors and borrowers become members of the society and have the right to say how the society is run. The Ecology Building Society is an authorised building society falling under the same statutory obligations as the high street giants. However, in its philosophy and reason for being it is very different from the better known societies.

Ideology

The Ecology Building Society was established in 1980 when an architect, an accountant, a solicitor and a printer were having a discussion on ecological issues. Their conversation turned to the narrow view some-times taken by building societies regarding loans on certain types of property. In cases where there was a lot of renovation work required. most lenders either applied high retention rates or would not release any of the loan at all until all the renovation work was completed. This meant that borrowers had to instruct contractors to carry out the work and incur high charges on bridging finance, which deterred many people from buying such properties.

The founders of the Ecology Building Society felt that this way of doing things encouraged the wasteful use of natural resources, such as new timber, and believed that the new society should make it possible for the borrowers to carry out the work themselves, using recycled materials where available. Many building societies were sceptical about helping people seeking to become self-reliant and would not help in the purchase of properties such as smallholdings and craft workshops. Energy-efficient homes such as back-to-back terrace houses in inner city areas were considered poor security, so loans were not always forth-coming to purchase these. Into this situation came the Ecology Building Society with its declared philosophy and unique lending policy. Written into the Rules of the Society is the following:

Rule 13 (1)   Advances shall be made to persons or on properties which, in the opinion of the Board, are most likely to lead to the saving of non-renewable energy resources, the promotion of self-sufficiency in individuals and communities, or the most ecologically efficient use of land.

A further rule states that for the rule above to be altered a majority vote of the whole membership of the Society must be obtained. It cannot therefore be changed by a small minority faction who may wish to alter the way in which the Society operates.

The following examples give a greater indication of what Rule 13 (1) means in practice.

The saving of non-renewable energy resources

A wind-powered turbine

Douglas and Sally purchased a remote house with some land in Scotland. There was no electricity, and power was being obtained from a petrol driven generator. The Ecology Building Society was able to help them purchase the property and a wind-powered turbine, thus saving non-renewable energy resources.

Roger and Margaret wanted to purchase a large Victorian house for themselves and others to live in and to use productively. Because of the property's design, heat was lost rapidly, particularly through the roof. As part of the Ecology Building Society's lending terms, insulation is required to a specific level. Roger found bargain insulation at their local DIY supermarket so he bought double the required amount and their roof is now insulated to a thickness of 200 mm rather than the usual 100 mm. They also installed a system whereby bath water from the first floor bathroom is stored and used to flush the ground floor toilet.

Pat built a cow byre onto her farmhouse. On top of the byre she constructed a greenhouse which was heated in the winter by the warmth generated by the cows. When she sold this house, she built another, again with a mortgage from the Ecology Building Society, and this time filled the concrete foundation with empty bottles. This had a great insulating effect, which will save a lot of heat in the years ahead.

Self-sufficiency

Two young women have been helped by the Ecology Building Society with a mortgage to run their business, Green Ark. They produce herbal remedies for animals and animal feed which is free from harmful additives. Their business has been instrumental in creating jobs in a rural area. Others have borrowed funds from the Society to start vegetarian restaurants, wholefood shops and hotels.

As well as individuals who have benefited from the Ecology Building Society's policies there are a number of groups such as housing co-operatives and workers' co-operatives which have not been able to find finance elsewhere. One in Hull, Giroscope, purchases run-down properties and renovates them as housing for those who would not be able to find a home otherwise. This group is serving a community as well as bringing back into use housing which might otherwise be demolished and lost from the housing stock.

The most ecologically efficient use of land

The Ecology Building Society is most concerned that investors' funds are used wisely, and to this end will not use money where it is not serving an ecologically sound purpose. The Society will not lend to those who wish to use the money to purchase a second home or a holiday cottage, and prefer to lend on land which is to be used productively. For example, loans will be made on land for use as a smallholding rather than for an ornamental garden. Land is a precious commodity, and must be used wisely if the planet is to continue to sustain human life.

A typical smallholding

The investors

The question could well be asked, 'Are ethical investors being exploited?' In the early years the Ecology Building Society needed to charge its borrowers interest 1.25 per cent above that charged by the major lenders. During the past five years this differential has been reduced to the point where the interest is only a fraction over the main lenders' rates. As a small enterprise the Society is not able to compete with the major building societies who make a great deal of their profit from subsidiary businesses. However, the basic accounts compare favourably and the higher interest accounts are not far behind. Many investors are prepared to forfeit a little interest to know that their money is being used in a way they consider sensible. The commitment of this Society is impressive. More members come to the Annual General Meeting than attend some of the very large societies' meetings. At these meetings there is a strong feeling of involvement. Members ask very pertinent questions. Business is discussed openly and frankly, and people travel many miles to be present and make their contribution.

The staff and their working environment

The staff and premises of the Society also reflect the Society's philosophy. Biodegradable cleaning products are used. Energy-efficient lighting has been introduced, recycled paper is used for all the Society's stationery and marketing literature and waste paper is sent for recycling.

The Board at present comprises three executive and five non-executive directors. Each has a specific contribution to make, ranging from computer programming to advice on smallholding. The directors' fees are minimal and for many years did not even cover travel expenses to board meetings.

Recognition

How do other building societies regard the Ecology Building Society? At first there was some cynicism and doubt about whether the fledgling society would survive. But as the Society began to grow in size and strength, support and help was offered by the big societies. One big society helps out in a practical way by allowing one of their local auditors to carry out the same job for the Ecology Building Society without making a charge. The Chief Executive of the Ecology Building Society has been invited on a number of occasions to address groups of building society personnel.

In practical terms, although the Society is value-led rather than profit-led, a degree of financial success has been achieved. The Society says that sound ecological sense means sound economic sense, and this is being proved as time goes on. The ecological approach can be cost-effective and certainly does not cost the earth!

Cosmetics To Go by Constantine and Weir PLC

Cosmetics To Go is the mail-order arm of cosmetic manufacturers Constantine and Weir PLC. It produces cruelty-free and biodegradable products suitable for use by vegetarians and environmentalists. In its present form it has been trading for four years although the parent company has been working with herbal hair and beauty products for 15 years. Constantine and Weir's turnover for the year 1990–1 was £7.3 million. Growth has been over 60 per cent each year over the last eight years. There are now 66 full-time and 25 part-time staff spread over three premises. The concept of a hierarchy is kept to a minimum: there are no directors' car park spaces and all company cars are available to all staff at all times. Despite their small size Constantine and Weir are taken very seriously by their competitors.

A selection of Cosmetics to Go products

The products are of a high quality. The wrapping reinforces the idea that cosmetics are luxuries to be enjoyed, and are about spoiling yourself. The considerable range of Cosmetics To Go products includes:

- natural moisturisers
- hand and body creams
- facial masks made with asparagus, garlic and lemon
- exfoliation bars
- soap wedges made from avocado, grapefruit, cinnamon, lime and aloe vera
- shampoo based on kelp, organic sulphur and juniper tar
- conditioners
- solid shampoo bars
- shaving creams
- protective blockers designed for extreme weather conditions.

Fresh ingredients such as vegetables and fruit are often used and preservatives are kept to a minimum. The company only uses cruelty-free testing methods. A further characteristic of Constantine and Weir is that the company is very open in its dealings; information concerning ingredients and production methods is freely available. The catalogue discusses in detail the ingredients of each product.

Eight rules

The company operates around eight basic rules to which staff are introduced on joining. These eight rules are part of the everyday running of the company and apply equally to managers and staff. They have grown out of years of experience.

Value people before profit

Although it is a business, Constantine and Weir focuses on people, both staff and customers. Typically, their customers are inquisitive and assertive and appreciate the company's open and approachable style. This motivates everyone involved in the company. The culture of the company facilitates staff involvement in all aspects of the business. The company operates a profit-sharing scheme for employees of more than two years standing: all employees receive the same amount regardless of status. The company also provides a pension and a health scheme and a well-stocked kitchen in every building. Constantine and Weir aim to provide job security, regarding staff as a valuable asset.

Develop and promote talent from within

Everyone joining the company starts with the knowledge that they are expected to be flexible and work in various areas of the company. Their reward for this is self-development and a comprehensive understanding of how the company works.

The company believes strongly in staff training. The directors believe that the business can only develop as the staff develop. Training covers health and development, as well as general education. It takes the form of a full timetable of 16 lectures a month organised and given by staff on subjects ranging from business French to homoeopathy and reflexology. External residential training is also encouraged for many members of staff, alongside company training days and programmes. Training is open to all employees, including those working part-time, and is flexible to requests.

Take responsibility for our environment

The company believes that it should try to set examples and raise awareness of environmental issues. Instances of this include the use of recycled paper for stationery, packaging and printed materials, the commissioning of energy audits to see where natural resources can be conserved and the development of new packaging from vegetable sources with the aim of replacing plastics. The company's profile says:

'As a company we are deeply concerned about the way the environment is being totally devastated by the industrial nations of the world for short-term profit. We believe it is possible to operate a profitable manufacturing company without risking our local and global environment . . .'

The following environmental questions are asked about all aspects of the business.

- Alternatives: is there an alternative which is commercially viable and environmentally kind?

- Buying: am I contributing to a destructive industry or process by buying this?

- Carriage: how can the product be transported with minimum effect on the environment?

- Disposal of packaging: is packaging available in biodegradable form? Can it be recycled?

- Effects: what effects will my actions have on the environment?

Value and serve our customers

The overriding feeling at Constantine and Weir is that the customer pays the wages, and as a result the company gives a great deal of attention to what the customers have to say, to the extent that they can legitimately claim to be customer led. Strict vegetarians, vegans and those concerned with testing procedures are served by the Cosmetics To Go catalogue. The company endeavours to fulfil orders as quickly and efficiently as possible and distributes questionnaires to its customers to monitor quality of product and service. It organises 'roadshows' which tour the country giving demonstrations and meeting customers. Of course, one of the best ways of guaranteeing customer satisfaction is to ensure the excellence of the products. All ingredients are of a high standard, the packaging is designed to be fun and new products are constantly introduced.

Benefit from the use of technology

Cosmetics To Go are largely a mail-order company so new technology is well used. From the ordering and invoicing right through to the quality control, computer-based systems are used to improve the efficiency of service to the customer.

All staff are encouraged to become familiar with as many different machines as possible. There are no secretaries so all staff must be able to use a word processing package. A recent skills audit showed that all staff could word process a letter and use a spreadsheet effectively. This leads to efficiency and a greater level of personal responsibility and has also helped to counter early and inaccurate perceptions of the company as a 'bunch of hippies'.

Create a balanced and profitable business

The company is aware of the obligation it has to its employees to remain in business and so avoid redundancies. As a manufacturer and retailer Constantine and Weir is able to develop in a way that is not dependent on a particular line of cosmetics and so should survive any drop in demand. There is an awareness that forward planning is essential for staff job security, and investments have been made in staff training so the company and its employees will be able to change if this is necessary. An example of forward planning is the way in which the company coped with the recession of the early 1990s. Taking action on projections in the mid 1980s, Constantine and Weir gradually reduced their staff, purely by natural wastage, from 90 to the present 66 full-time, thus safeguarding jobs and the future of the company.

The company is aware that it could easily double its staff and factory space, but does not feel that this would lead to a proportional growth in quality of service and productivity. Further, it does not want to lose the personal, friendly and co-operative atmosphere it has created, and the obvious commitment and loyalty of staff.

Behave ethically

'From the tea we drink to the companies we deal with, we are trying to boycott any product or producer whose trading falls below an accepted level. The other side of this sees us giving our support to companies and products that we consider to have sound, eco-kind attitudes towards their business.' (Cosmetics To Go company profile)

The Cosmetics to Go catalogue

The company has always tried to operate ethically and has always asked, 'How can we be honourable to our customers, our staff and ourselves?' This has meant making new ethical decisions as the company has grown, as ethical goalposts have changed, and as customer requirements have changed.

Testing cosmetics to see if they are comfortable and safe for humans to use has always been of prime concern to the company. The company have developed their own Assisi project, named after St Francis of Assisi, the patron saint of animals.

This involves the use of a panel of volunteers. All Cosmetics To Go products carry the slogan 'Tested on humans for irritancy'.

Communicate effectively

As well as team meetings, the company holds small group meetings every fortnight where staff of all levels meet to discuss their concerns and the progress of the company generally. Constructive criticism is encouraged. Ford Motor Company President, Lee Iacocca said, 'We need to care about each other and help others'. This is wholeheartedly endorsed at Cosmetics To Go. Effective communication at work is further aided by the activities organized by the company outside working hours. As well as training there are sports days, Christmas shopping trips and firework nights, usually attended by the whole company.

The mail order catalogue by which the company communicates with customers tries to be an honest summation of the products available and tries to present an accurate picture of the company as approachable and concerned.

Constantine and Weir are an equal opportunities employer and have won an award for 'Women Mean Business'. Women have been appointed in ares such as production and forklift driving which has confounded some of the male drivers making deliveries who keep asking for the storeman. Four out of the seven directors are women.

The company is very careful about the ingredients it uses. For example, only free range eggs are used. Great care is taken to include only ingredients of benefit to the user. Their catalogues do not sell cosmetics as items essential to beauty and romantic or sexual success, rather they stress feeling good about yourself and having fun.

An excerpt from the Cosmetics to Go catalogue

Constantine and Weir is very self-critical. For example, in a training video, 'Customers First', they interviewed dissatisfied customers. The video serves as a stark and sobering reminder to all staff of the areas in which the company needs to develop.

Constantine and Weir have proved that a business can operate with principles and be successful. Their success can be attributed to a combination of business acumen, openness, honesty and a genuine concern for staff and customers.

Now that you've looked at two organisations who try to implement ethical principles, look at the fictitious company of Harwoods Soft Drinks and try to make responsible decisions for them.

The case-study company: a profile

Harwoods Soft Drinks PLC
Harwood House
Milestone Road
Rolfham
MR17 8GH

History

Joseph Harwood, Canned Soft Drinks Manufacturers, has approximately 1000 employees on several sites throughout the north of England. Originally a sole trader, Harwood started just after the war making drinks in a small way from home. The business grew quickly, and to raise extra capital for more factory premises, Harwood issued shares in the company. As a PLC it developed a sophisticated organisational structure. Nevertheless, as Chairman, Harwood always adopted a strong patriarchal role, making all important decisions himself. He was always genuinely concerned about the welfare of his staff.

The company held a major market share in the north of England in the soft drinks industry. The range included: lemonade, orangeade, colas, diet drinks and fruit juices.

When he recently suffered a major stroke, Joseph Harwood allowed the company to be the subject of a takeover by the American multinational, Leisure Products Inc., and he retired. It is now in a period of transition. Harwoods was an attractive proposition for Leisure Products Inc. because it had built up a solid market, which complemented their own range of drinks. A further attraction of Harwoods Soft Drinks was that it owned a canning plant and imported all its own raw materials, both for manufacturing the drinks and for producing standard tin cans.

Current situation

Leisure Products Inc. is a dynamic, go-ahead enterprise which considers that Joseph Harwood's business needs to be modernised. J Edmund

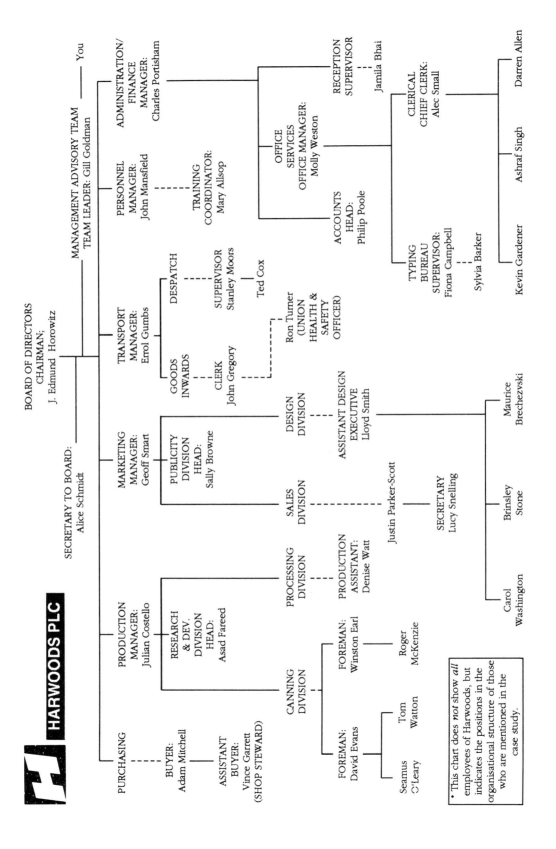

HARWOODS PLC

BOARD OF DIRECTORS
CHAIRMAN;
J. Edmund Horowitz

SECRETARY TO BOARD:
Alice Schmidt

MANAGEMENT ADVISORY TEAM
TEAM LEADER: Gill Goldman ——— You

PURCHASING

BUYER:
Adam Mitchell

ASSISTANT
BUYER:
Vince Garrett
(SHOP STEWARD)

PRODUCTION
MANAGER:
Julian Costello

RESEARCH
& DEV.
DIVISION
HEAD:
Asad Fareed

CANNING
DIVISION

PROCESSING
DIVISION

FOREMAN:
David Evans

Seamus
O'Leary

Tom
Watton

FOREMAN:
Winston Earl

Roger
McKenzie

PRODUCTION
ASSISTANT:
Denise Watt

MARKETING
MANAGER:
Geoff Smart

PUBLICITY
DIVISION
HEAD:
Sally Browne

SALES
DIVISION

DESIGN
DIVISION

ASSISTANT DESIGN
EXECUTIVE
Lloyd Smith

Justin Parker-Scott

SECRETARY
Lucy Snelling

Carol
Washington

Brinsley
Stone

Maurice
Brechezvski

TRANSPORT
MANAGER:
Errol Gumbs

GOODS
INWARDS

CLERK
John Gregory

DESPATCH

SUPERVISOR
Stanley Moors

Ted Cox

Ron Turner
(UNION
HEALTH &
SAFETY
OFFICER)

PERSONNEL
MANAGER:
John Mansfield

TRAINING
COORDINATOR:
Mary Allsop

ADMINISTRATION/
FINANCE
MANAGER:
Charles Portisham

OFFICE
SERVICES
OFFICE MANAGER:
Molly Weston

RECEPTION
SUPERVISOR

Jamila Bhai

ACCOUNTS
HEAD:
Philip Poole

TYPING
BUREAU
SUPERVISOR:
Fiona Campbell

Sylvia Barker

CLERICAL
CHIEF CLERK:
Alec Small

Kevin Gardener

Ashraf Singh

Darren Allen

• This chart does *not* show *all* employees of Harwoods, but indicates the positions in the organisational structure of those who are mentioned in the case study.

Horowitz, Chairperson of Leisure Products Inc., has been quoted as saying, 'This company needs a good kick into the nineties.' He recognises that Harwood was a good, if idiosyncratic, employer, who looked after his staff and was aware of his obligations. However, it is his wish that his newly acquired British subsidiary should become more efficient and more socially responsible, in line with American models. Furthermore, he is keen to exploit the opportunity to enter the European market. He is aware that Harwoods Soft Drinks will have to operate according to European guidelines on pollution, marketing and staff management.

Therefore, in the wake of Harwood's departure, Leisure Products Inc. are planning to create new policies and operational procedures to act as guidelines for decision makers in the organisation. To achieve this they have set up a management advisory team, based at the Rolfham head office. The brief of the team is to adapt and update existing policy, as well as to create new directives and review unusual situations.

Your role

You are a member of this management advisory team, headed by the dynamic Gill Goldman, who established herself as one of the company's top people by creating strategies for expanding into the Third World market.

Your skills have given you the opportunity to handle problems, either on your own, or by referring up the organisation. The job often requires you to check on facts, sum up the pros and cons of situations and give your opinions.

You find the following documents in your in-tray for your attention. They come from a variety of people within the organisation, customers and business contacts.

As you would find in an office situation, the documents are in no particular order with regard to content or importance. Therefore you will need to scan all the documents before beginning any specific task you are asked to do.

In-tray exercises: 1
Personnel

When working through these memos, think about the following points.

- Most companies care about the welfare of their staff, but the overall aim is to make a profit so that the company can keep going. How do managers balance the two goals of making money and keeping a happy staff? Are the two goals incompatible?
- The individual staff in any company will have different backgrounds, needs, ambitions and personalities. The company must co-ordinate these very different people in an efficient way and must smooth any problems that arise. The examples show that this is often difficult.
- How far does taking good care of staff pay for itself in producing better motivated, more loyal staff? If you think it does achieve this, consider whether prioritising staff welfare is an ethical decision or a management strategy for motivating staff. Does the thinking matter if the end is the same?
- Why do organisations train their staff? Remember how costly training is, both in terms of the resources needed and the productive working time lost. Well trained staff may then leave the organisation to work for a competitor. Has their training been a waste of money for a) the company b) the staff member? If not, why not?
- What rights do you think staff should have? What say should they have about working conditions, management decisions, and access to information? Is it part of a union's role to protect these rights?

Case 1

To: Gill Goldman
From: Alice Schmidt
Date: 25.1.9–
Subject: HIV testing

We have received the attached letter from Preston General Insurance.
Do you think we could introduce HIV testing? Would the unions
object?

If we decide not to opt for testing, we'll have to find new insurers. If
we decide to introduce a testing scheme, how should it be organised?

I'd be grateful for your thoughts as soon as possible.

Alice Schmidt

19.1.9–

Mr C Portisham
Harwoods
Harwood House
Milestone Road
Rolfham

Preston General Insurance PLC
Merchant House
Preston
PN4 9UH

Our ref. PR/ke

Dear Mr Portisham

Company Healthsafe Insurance Scheme

As you will recall, you have a policy in this scheme for the benefit of Harwoods' senior staff. It is now time for the annual renewal premium to be paid, and this seems a good time to review your company's healthcare needs.

The existing scheme provides private hospital treatment of unlimited duration, private nursing home stay for up to two months after hospitalisation, and private out-patient consultations.

These benefits are available to all Harwoods' management staff who have been with the company for a minimum of one year. You will be aware that these benefits are more generous than those currently being offered by competitors in the healthcare insurance market, and we are pleased to inform you that the current low premium levels are being maintained for this year.

However, in order to ensure that we can keep the premiums low, it is necessary for us to limit the risks of substantial claims. At present your employees are offered automatic acceptance into the scheme without a medical examination. From next year, cover will be offered only to those employees who are tested HIV negative. In the light of this change, you may wish to review your employment application procedures if you are not currently checking that all staff are HIV negative. It must be stressed that your insurance cover would be void if such staff were included in the policy with, or without, your knowledge.

I trust you will take the necessary steps to ensure that this excellent insurance cover can continue to be provided for all your management staff, and should be pleased to answer any further queries you may have on the policy.

Yours sincerely

G W Henderson (Policy Services Manager)

Issues raised

This letter raises questions about how much medical and personal information an employer is entitled to know about his employees, and about fringe benefits.

Increasingly, insurance companies are asking questions about lifestyle in order to assist them in calculating the risks, particularly on life assurance and medical cover insurance policies.

Will having been tested for HIV discriminate unfairly against applicants for jobs? Is it fair, or accurate, to make assumptions about a person's sex life if they admit to having been tested for the HIV virus? Will people applying for jobs answer such questions honestly when they fill in application forms?

There is a dilemma here, for the employer needs this information if he is to be able to continue providing this healthcare protection for his existing staff.

Group medical insurance policies cost significantly less than the individual would pay if he arranged similar insurance cover for himself. Thus, participation in a company private medical insurance scheme is a financial benefit to the employee as well as a recruitment incentive to the company. However, should companies offer such fringe benefits, or simply pay proportionately higher salaries? Is private medical care acceptable in principle, if it means some people receive better or quicker service than others because they can pay for it?

Case 2

To: Gill Goldman
From: Julian Costello
Date: 23.2.9–
Subject: Workers with a disability

I have just received this note from Denise Watt. Do we have any consistent policy towards disabled workers? We now have quite a few people with special needs in the workforce.

Should we put some ramps in the canteen? What modifications are needed to the showers? How much would it all cost?

I'd be grateful for some guidance as soon as possible. Do you want to have a word with Denise yourself?

Julian Costello.

---

14 Ash Road
Rolfham

Dear Mr Costello,

I work on the shop floor in the Juice Processing Division. I recently returned to work after a motorcycle accident in which I lost part of my right leg below the knee.

I find it almost impossible to reach the canteen or the showers without help. I don't want to be a burden, and I can do my job as well as before as I now have an artificial limb. I just want to be able to move around the factory like I could before. Can you help?

Yours sincerely
Denise Watt

Issues raised

Are you surprised that this worker is a woman? Does it affect your judgement of the situation?

Denise is obviously fit for work and doing her job as well as before.

The memo points out that Harwoods have been negligent in dealing with disabled access/facilities for the disabled. What should they do? What are their legal obligations? How should they start redressing the inequality? They could ask those presently disadvantaged to suggest improvements.

Notice Julian Costello's lack of knowledge and confusion. Does the management need consciousness-raising sessions on all kinds of disability? Do they need introducing to the idea of the responsible company?

Julian asks about the cost of modifying the plant to make it easier for disabled people to move about. Do you think he is most concerned with people or profit? How do you think managers strike a balance between caring for their staff and keeping the finances of the company healthy?

Case 3

To: Gill Goldman
From: Mary Allsop, Training Coordinator,
      Personnel Department
Date: 10.3.9–
Subject: Staff Training

As you requested, I have monitored the staff induction courses run last month, and report the following reactions from new staff.

Ninety per cent were generally satisfied with the length and content of the course. Fifty per cent were dissatisfied with Health and Safety aspects, saying more information was needed on this topic.

I am therefore currently looking for a suitable film or video to teach new staff about Health and Safety laws which affect the workplace. Could one of your staff help me? I need a list of suppliers of video training material with a breakdown of costs.

Many thanks.

Mary Allsop.

Issues raised

Why do companies provide induction training for staff?

This memo notes that the staff were unhappy about the Health and Safety aspect of induction. Will showing a video be the best way to improve coverage? It could be seen as a cost cutting/cheap way of dealing with the issue. As it is non-participative and a passive form of learning, is it likely to be effective? What do you think would be a better method? How important is thorough Health and Safety training?

See memo from Charles Portisham on the budget cuts. Are savings in this area legitimate?

Case 4

To: Fiona Campbell, Typing Bureau
From: John Mansfield, Personnel
Date: 13.4.9–
Subject: Clerk/Typist Vacancy – Typing Pool

I have received only three suitable applications for this post which we advertised last week in the local press. Would you let me know whether you wish to interview these applicants immediately in view of the urgency of filling the vacancy left by Mrs Barker's retirement.

Summary for comparison

Name	
	Miss Jenny Snowden
Age	17
Qualifications	GCSE English E, Cookery D, Geography E, French E
	RSA Typewriting 1, Office Practice 1, Communications 2
Work experience	Saturday job at the local supermarket since January
Health	Generally good.

Name	Mrs Deidre Snow
Age	45
Qualifications	RSA Typewriting 3, Shorthand 3
Employment	Various clerical and secretarial jobs. Currently part-time clerk/typist at British Gas
Health	Generally good
	Wishes to return to full-time employment
	Has three children, aged 6, 9 and 12.

Name	Mr Juan Campbell
Age	21
Qualifications	GCSE English 3, RSA Typewriting 2
Employment	Various temporary jobs in offices and hotels
Health	Good. Wheelchair.

John Mansfield

Issues raised

In what way does this memo highlight stereotyping; Juan is disabled, perhaps with a Latin background, and male. Would you discount him from the post with these points in mind? Does Harwoods need an Equal Opportunities monitoring system for job applications? (See p. 72 for an example.)

The memo also raises the issue of women returners. Many companies now make positive steps to employ those returning to employment after raising a family. Should the company have such a policy?

In terms of qualifications Mrs Snow is the best candidate. Should these be the only criteria for selection?

Who would you recommend for the vacancy? Why? Is your decision justifiable?

Case 5

To: Gill Goldman
From: John Mansfield
Date: 20.4.9–
Subject: Dismissal

Will you please check the legal position for me on dismissing staff?

There's a pretty, young girl in the typing pool who has only been with us for six months, but she has already complained on several occasions to Molly Weston about unwelcome sexual advances from a very senior member of staff. The easiest thing to do would be to dismiss her. Can I do this, or is it unfair dismissal?

Issues raised

Is the suggested action legal? Do your management staff know about the laws governing sexual discrimination and unfair dismissal? If not, how could their understanding of the issues be increased?

In this instance, what action would you recommend? You could suggest that the woman is moved to fill the clerk/typist vacancy (see memo 4), but this may mean she is further disadvantaged by the harassment. Would that be fair?

One idea might be to find out who is being accused of sexual harassment, and find someone senior to him to have an informal discussion about the matter. What would you do if he is the most senior member of staff?

In the future would it be advisable, or legal, to ensure a man is appointed to replace this girl?

Case 6

To: Gill Goldman
From: Julian Costello
Date: 21:5:9—
Subject: Attached Memo

I received this from Winston Earl. What do you think? Roger's been with us for 10 years, so I am reluctant to dismiss him, but there really is no suitable job for him in our section. Do you think you could find him work in another department? If not, what are the options? Dismissal, redundancy or what?

Julian Costello.

To: Julian Costello, Production Manager
From: Winston Earl, Foreman
Date: 19.5.9—

You remember that Roger McKenzie, one of my staff in the juice extraction section, was involved in a car accident a month ago. He returned to work this Monday, but I don't know what work I can give him to do. His right hand is useless – paralysed permanently he says – so he can't do his usual work at all. He used to operate the machines and was responsible for checking their accuracy and adjusting the pressure. This job needs pretty good manual control and he can't do it with his left hand. Actually I daren't let him near the machines as he's not safe to operate them. So please let me know what work I can give him to do. Thanks. Winston Earl.

Issues raised

Obviously Harwoods have an unproductive employee here and cannot afford to continue paying him for doing nothing. So what are the alternatives for the company?

- Are there any grounds on which he could be dismissed?
- What are the legal rights of an employee who becomes unfit to perform the job for which he was employed?
- Do Harwoods have either a legal or a moral obligation to find Roger some alternative employment?
- Why might they decide to keep him on their payroll?

Case 7

To: Gill Goldman
From: Lloyd Smith, Assistant Design
    Executive, Marketing
Date: 6.6.9–
Subject: Post of Assistant Design Executive

You will recall that I will be moving from my present post to take up the post of Senior Creative Director. Personnel asked me to put something in writing about the suitability of my two deputies who are both applying for the vacancy this will create.

Carol Washington is a good all-round worker with drive and enthusiasm. However she does require some time off as she is bringing up two children on her own. She takes time off if they are sick and sometimes in the school holidays and leaves early in term time to meet them from school. However she always works through her lunch hour to make up the time, and her qualifications are excellent.

Brinsley Stone is a fair worker too. Like Carol he is dedicated, but perhaps without her flair, although he too has good qualifications. I would have to recommend Brinsley purely on the absence issue.

Issues raised

This is a potential case of sexual discrimination. Carol is probably the better candidate, but is being discounted by her superior as she is a mother. However, remember that Lloyd Smith is only offering advice, not taking a decision, so Carol could be appointed despite his resistance.

Should Carol's family circumstances be taken into account in deciding her suitability for promotion? What problems are her absences and irregular working hours likely to cause the company?

If Harwoods decide she is the better candidate and ought to be appointed how might they cope with the problem her situation causes?

This memo raised the general issue of flexible working hours and flexitime. Flexitime is very popular with workers. Why do you think this is? Why do you think companies might introduce flexitime, and why might they oppose its introduction?

Case 8

To: Gill Goldman
From: Adam Mitchell
Date: 12.9.9–

I found this notice on the staff notice board. What's going on? Do we recognise the FAAIU (Food and Allied Industries Union)? When was Vince elected shop steward? How many members has the union recruited? Can they hold a meeting in working hours?

i hope you will investigate and report back as soon as possible. I think we should come down hard on the Union – we don't want the unions to start running our business.

Adam Mitchell

FAAIU

FAAIU MEMBERS

There will be a meeting for all FAAIU members on Tuesday 1 September at 4 pm in the works canteen.

Please make every effort to attend as *your* Union needs *your* support. We will be discussing pay and conditions, as well as the new membership drive.

Vince Garrett, Shop Steward

Issues raised

Points to think about here are concerned with the relationship between unions and management. The writer of the note is clearly not sympathetic to the Union's activities.

- Is he correct to query a meeting held during working hours?
- Why do you think he is hostile to the Union?
- Why might management welcome the existence of a trade union representing their workforce?
- Why do trade unions exist and are they necessary?
- What do they achieve that benefits the workers, the management and the industry?

Are you a member of your Student Union? What are the similarities and differences between the Student Union and an industrial union?

Case 9

To: Gill Goldman
From: Charles Portisham, Administration
        Manager
Date: 5.1.9–
Subject: Budget 199–

The budget allocations for the coming financial year are to be
reapportioned as follows:

Publicity and Advertising   +10%
Pollution Control   −5%
Staff Training   −5%

Other allocations remain unchanged from the last financial year.
These changes are proposed on the grounds that:
a) increased advertising is needed to maintain our market share;
b) publicity is needed to promote our new image since the takeover;
c) satisfactory levels of pollution control have been achieved at the
   canning factory;
d) the staff appraisal system has identified wastage in training
   programmes;
e) Personnel recommend shorter induction courses for new staff.

Please let me have your observations on these allocations before I
present them formally to the Board of Directors at their meeting in
two weeks' time.

Charles Portisham

Issues raised

The important points to note here are that the company has intended to
cut the budget on staff training and on pollution control. There are
sufficient examples within the rest of the case-study to see clearly that
staff could be more aware of Health and Safety issues. Given the letter to
The Reporter on litter in the town (see Case 32) it may be fair to suggest
that there is equal feeling about the environment.

Does the company want to be responsible for more pollution? It may
be open to bad publicity if it is found out that it is cutting the budget
here. Is there a conflict of interests within the company between
balancing the budget and cutting costs and in acting in a more ethical
and environmentally friendly way?

Refer to Case 3 from Mary Allsop, Training Coordinator.

Case 10

To: Gill Goldman
From: John Mansfield, Personnel
Date: 30.9.9–

With reference to the attached memo, do you think we should make it company policy to offer early retirement to all staff over 55 ? Cox has been with us 23 years and given good service, but now his wife is sick and he's obviously feeling the strain. If he went we could employ somebody younger, keener and stronger. A young person could also be paid less than Ted, who's accumulated so many long service increments. Let me know what you think and I'll have a word with Ted on his return.

To: John Mansfield, Personnel
From: Stanley Moors, Supervisor,
　　　 Dispatch Department
Date: 27.9.9–
Subject: Staffing

On August 10 Ted Cox was absent from work with a headache. Then August 15–28 he was off again, this time with a doctor's note about stress. Now he is away again and has been off all this week. All this absence makes it difficult for me to run the department properly. I think Ted is just waiting to retire – after all he's 57. Will you have a word with him when he comes back as he's really not pulling his weight.

Thanks.

Issues raised

Cox features in a possible racist attack discussed later on (see Case 19). Would you consider dismissal? On what grounds?

There is the issue of early retirement; can it be enforced? Cox has been a good worker but his work has recently deteriorated, possibly due to his wife's poor health. Should the company try to help him? Is there the facility in the company to do this? Can the company say it helps its staff?

This memo can also be used to question the ethics of employing younger people who can be paid less money to do the same job as an older, more expensive, worker. Does this make sense from the company's point of view?

Case 11

To: Gill Goldman
From: Vince Garrett, Union rep
Date: 10.7.9–

My members have recently expressed concern that the records kept in personnel have been put onto computer. Who has access to the computer? How will we be able to check our records. How will the records be corrected, if wrong, and how will they be used?

Vince Garrett

Issues raised

What right do people have to control information about themselves? Do they have different rights with respect to different types of information (medical records, personnel files) and with respect to different organisations (the state, the police, the company)?

What sort of information do different organisations hold about you? Have you seen all your records? Do you want to? Could you gain access to such information to check it?

Investigate the provisions of the Data Protection Act.

In-tray exercises: 2 Ethical investment and ethical consumerism

Refer back to the introduction for detailed information about ethical investment and ethical consumerism. When working through the memos in this section, think about the points below.

- When a company purchases raw materials e.g. food for the canteen, company cars, office supplies, machinery, etc. it is a consumer of someone else's product. Should it consider how ethically that product has been made? e.g. how environmentally friendly the production process was, how recyclable the product is, whether the people involved in its production were fairly treated.
- Similarly, when an organisation has money to invest e.g. in a pension scheme for its employees, it is a consumer of another company's product. Should it simply look for an investment scheme which brings the highest financial return? Or does it have a responsibility to ensure that other people are not being exploited to gain this profit?
- All PLCs with shares on the Stock Exchange are required by law to publish an annual report. These reports are widely available, and will tell you something of where a company invests and how it conducts its business. Look at the annual report of a PLC which interests you.

Case 12

To: Gill Goldman
From: Charles Portisham
Date: 20.8.9–

With reference to the attached letter, do we know how our pension funds are invested at the moment? I think we ought to explore the ethical investment movement and come up with a company policy. We could then make a statement to staff, in case any of them feel strongly about this. Could you set things in motion and get back to me within six weeks?

Many thanks.

Charles Portisham

HAMPSON, AZIZ AND TRUPPORT

Chiswick High Road
London W4

Independent Investment Advisors

Date: 16.8.9

ref. PH/SAW

Mr C Portisham
Harwoods
Harwood House
Milestone Road
Rolfham

Dear Mr Portisham

We have recently received several telephone calls from concerned shareholders of yours. This follows a recent episode of the Channel 4 programme *Company Law* which investigated the companies, industries, and countries in which PLCs invest for their pension schemes.

Your shareholders, two in particular who own substantial amounts, are interested in whether we invest, on your behalf, in the following:

1. companies with any armaments or defence connections
2. countries with poor human rights records
3. companies who unnecessarily exploit the Third World.

Do you have a policy on such matters? Now that the Ethical Investment movement has grown considerably we are able to offer you a choice of companies to invest in depending on how you wish to limit your investment. We would point out that some of these ethical investments do not provide the same high yield as more conventional investment sources.

Please instruct us accordingly.

Yours sincerely

Paul Hampton
Director

Issues raised

Do you agree with Portisham that Harwoods should have a policy on ethical investment? How could Gill investigate the alternative ethical investment movement? This is an area of tremendous recent growth. Ethical investment agencies guarantee that they do not invest in 'unethical' companies and countries, and are happy to declare where they do invest, unlike some agencies. They often have a statement similar to a mission statement concerning their investment priorities. This states where they will not invest, for example, in areas such as arms companies, countries with poor human rights records etc.

Again a good public image can be developed if the company can show that it is investing ethically.

Ethical investments may not produce high returns. Should Harwoods simply choose investments which yield the greatest profit?

Why do you think Portisham was concerned to make a policy statement to staff?

Case 13

To: Gill Goldman
From: Asad Fareed,
      Head of Research and Development
Date: 17.9.9–

It has come to my attention that one of our aluminium suppliers is wholly owned by a South American parent company with a disgraceful human rights record, e.g. exploiting child labour, brutal discipline, unhygienic working conditions and a reputation for exploiting the rainforests (one of its other interests is timber). Do you think I ought to start exploring alternative suppliers?

I am unhappy that Harwoods is giving business to, and boosting the profits of, this dubious company. Do we have a company-wide policy on such matters?

Asad Fareed

Issues raised

In this example Harwoods is acting as a consumer. Asad Fareed is concerned that the company should act as an ethical consumer. What issues do you think the managers would need to investigate before formulating a policy on ethical consumerism?

Amongst other things, they would need to investigate whether the allegations against the aluminium supplier were true (how would they do this?) and the cost of alternative sources of supply. If the cost of buying aluminium elsewhere is enormous, do you think the company should be prepared to pay the extra money?

Case 14

To: Gill Goldman
From: Lloyd Smith
Date: 23.9.9–

It has come to my attention that at least two local dentists are advising parents not to buy our drinks for their children because, the dentists claim, the drinks contain a disproportionate amount of sugar and will rot children's teeth.

Have we any information to put out that would undermine the dentists' claim? We don't want people to stop buying our product.

Lloyd Smith.

Issues raised

This memo raises a number of issues, specifically that Harwoods manufactures a product which can lead to bad health. Soft drinks contain sugar which rots teeth, can cause obesity and is a nutrient-free source of energy. In an ideal world, do you think that unwholesome products would be allowed? If not, why not? If so, why?

If experts are advising consumers not to buy a particular product, under what circumstances should their advice be followed and under what circumstances should it be ignored? Have you ever stopped buying a product because experts advised it was bad for your health, or for any other reason?

More generally, this memo hints at the fact that Harwoods manufactures a useless product. Harwoods uses natural resources to produce something which people don't really need. What is the justification for this?

In-tray exercises: 3 Health and Safety

Health and safety issues have already been raised in Case 3 concerning staff training. Whilst working through the following cases you should pay special attention to the points below.

- Legally an employer has a responsibility to provide a safe and healthy working environment for staff. Even if the law did not require these standards of health and safety, why do you think an employer might take care to avoid exposing his/her employees to hazards, health risks, etc?
- Did you know that employees also have a legal duty to behave in such a way that they do not endanger the health and safety of any other staff? No doubt there are regulations at your school or college about behaviour. Do any relate to Health and Safety issues?
- Some health risks are obvious – e.g. trailing leads, improperly secured scaffolding, unprotected machinery, poisonous substances, etc. Others are only recognised as hazards after an accident has occurred – e.g. substances mislabelled, boxes blocking fire exits, furniture with sharp edges, etc.
- A newer type of hazard to be recognised is that which gradually causes damage to health – e.g. asbestos inhalation, eyestrain from overuse of VDUs, back injuries caused by lifting or poorly designed seating. This is called Repetitive Strain Injury. Staff in particular occupations may suffer more illnesses, and have more time off work, than do their colleagues. Consider the effect of this on their personnel record.
- Is smoking a Health and Safety issue?

As an interesting comparison with industrial attitudes to Health and Safety, it might be worth finding out about the Health and Safety policy of your college or school. If such a policy does not exist, ask why not. If it does exist, did you know the contents before you read this book? Find out as much as you can about the Health and Safety At Work Act.

Case 15

To: Gill Goldman
From: Julian Costello
Date: 21.9.9–

With reference to the two attached accident report forms please check
the Health and Safety at Work Act as Ron Turner is entitled to take us
to court over the missing machine guard and the state of the carpet if
we are at fault. However, both accidents happened on Friday
afternoon and I reckon O'Leary had been drinking at lunchtime –
Parker-Scott admits as much – so the accident could have been due to
an employee's own carelessness.

Whoever's to blame, do you think we ought to offer O'Leary
compensation? If so, how much? I don't think Parker-Scott deserves
anything as he admits drinking and was not badly hurt.

Please reply as soon as possible

Many thanks.

Julian Costello.

Accident Report Form

Name: Seamus O'Leary
Job Title: Machine Operator
Section/Dept: Canning
Extension: 372

Accident details
Date: Friday 17 October
Time: 2.15pm
Location   Canning section
Description of accident: Finger crushed by machine. No guard in position when making adjustment.

Witnessed by:
1. Name: Tom Walton   2. Name: David Evans
    Job Title: Machine Operator   Job Title: Foreman

Injuries: Finger crushed and needed amputation. Shock.
Medical attention: First-aid (Tom Walton). Casualty Department, Rolfham General Infirmary.
Absence from work: Doctor's certificate for one month

Signed D Evans

Accident Report Form

Name: Justin Parker-Scott
Job Title: Sales Manager
Section/Dept: Marketing
Extension: 194

Accident details

Date: Friday 31 October
Time: 2.30pm
Location   Stairs from reception to first floor
Description of accident: Had just got back to the office after lunch at the Ten Green Bottles (Lucy Snelling's leaving do) when I was bleeped. Went to answer on the phone at the top of the stairs, but I tripped on worn and uneven staircarpet. Fell very heavily on staircase.

Witnessed by:

1. Name: Lucy Snelling   2. Name: Jamila Bhai
    Job Title: Secretary   Job Title: Receptionist

Injuries: Bruised leg, twisted ankle, broken wrist.

Medical attention: Ankle bandaged by first-aider (Tom Walton) and wrist set in plaster at Rolfham General Infirmary.

Absence from work: Two weeks

Signed Justin Parker-Scott

Justin Parker - Scott

Issues raised

These forms raise a number of issues. In the first case, was the absence of the safety guard on the machinery the company's fault or the employee's fault? Would you blame the employee because of the time and the possibility that he had been drinking? If you would not blame the employee, but the company, give your reasons.

If you think the company is at fault, what remedies do you think need to be made? Is the Health and Safety induction course sufficient? See Case 9 on possible budget cuts here. If there was negligence on the part of the company, how would you make sure it did not happen again? What is the procedure for reporting accidents? Had it been followed here? Does the company have a departmental Safety Officer? Perhaps safety checks/inspection procedures need reviewing.

On the issue of compensation, how do you think the level of compensation would be decided? What price would you put on your own finger?

In the case of Parker-Scott, who do you think was most at fault? Parker-Scott, because he had been drinking, or the company, because of the carpet? Should the company replace the carpet? Is it a legal requirement that the company replace the carpet? Do you think Parker-Scott deserves any compensation? If so, why and how much?

If you were a union representative, how would you approach management on these safety issues? Why?

Incidentally, did you make any assumptions about these members of staff because of their names? If so, what assumptions and why did you make them?

Finally, make sure you are aware of the procedure for reporting an accident in your own school or college.

Case 16

To: Gill Goldman
From: Ron Turner, Health and Safety Officer
Date: 3.11.9–
Subject: Use of VDUs in accounting department

I am contacting you on behalf of the members of the FAAIU because we are very concerned about the company's attitude to VDUs. Overuse of VDUs can lead to eyestrain, and excessive use of the keyboard can lead to repetitive strain injuries (RSI).

We want workers in accounts, who use the screens all the time, to be allowed 10 minutes rest in every hour. Furthermore we want all female employees who become pregnant to be allowed to move to a department where VDUs are not in use, as radiation from the screens may harm unborn babies.

This is formal notification that an ergonomics expert from the Union head office will be visiting the accounts department next week to check that the seats, lighting and heights of desks are correct for prolonged VDU use. Poor seating, lighting and furniture can lead to all sorts of problems for workers.

Ron Turner

Issues raised

Do you think the Union is overreacting to the problems of VDU use?

Even if VDUs were shown to be perfectly safe for use by pregnant women, do you think such women should be allowed to change jobs within the company to guarantee peace of mind?

Do you think the Union was sensible simply to inform management that an ergonomics expert was coming in? Do you think there should have been negotiation about this before the memo was written? Do you think management would inform the union about a similar situation? If you think confrontation would arise, how do you consider it would best be handled? What sort of thing might the ergonomics expert recommend? Why might the company accept his/her recommendations? Why might it reject them? How much do you think it would cost to refurbish a medium sized accounts department to ensure all workstations were ergonomically designed? What are a company's legal obligations towards staff in respect of VDU use?

Case 17

> To: Gill Goldman
> From: Jamila Bhai, Reception Supervisor
> Date: 23.11.9–
>
> Gill, I received this petition about the state of the women's toilets. I think we should take action as soon as possible. Do you think we should get in some new cleaners?

Petition

We, the undersigned, are protesting about the state of the women's toilets on the back staircase. The toilets often get blocked-up, and there is frequently a horrible smell in there. The area round the sinks is always covered in dirty water and the floor is often littered with paper towels etc. One of the hand-driers has been broken for three weeks. Feeling is running very high about this.

[signatures]

Issues raised

The state of the toilets is a serious issue. There are health implications and it makes life very unpleasant for all users if the toilets are unsanitary.

Who do you think is responsible for the state of the toilets? Do you think there is a problem with the drains? If so, that is a problem for the maintenance department. Are the cleaners doing their job properly? If not, should they be replaced, or merely warned to improve their performance? How far can the users of the toilets be held responsible for the state they are in?

Feeling is obviously running high; what action would you take to calm everyone down?

Case 18

To: Gill Goldman
From: Molly Weston, Office Manager
Date: 15.12.9–

Can't something be done about the heating and/or the ventilation on the first floor? Everyone here either fries or freezes. There seems to be no middle ground. Please investigate.

Molly Weston .

Issues raised

Heating and ventilation are important for maintaining comfort and a healthy workforce. What problems can arise from poor heating and ventilation (you might also think about poor lighting)? What are a company's legal and moral obligations in these respects?

IN-TRAY EXERCISES: 4 EQUAL OPPORTUNITIES

What does Equal Opportunities mean? Does your college have an equal opportunities policy? What is it?

Whilst working through these exercises you should think about:

- The different groups for whom Equal Opportunities is a live issue: women, people with special needs (the mentally disadvantaged and physically disabled), homosexuals, the elderly, people with distinct cultural backgrounds, those from abroad, those whose skin is a different colour, people who observe strict religious practices and everyone else who is traditionally disadvantaged.
- Legally employers should treat all staff, and applicants for jobs, in exactly the same way, regardless of their sex, race, etc. In practice this is often difficult and costly to enforce.
- How realistic is it to expect everyone to be treated equally in the workplace? How desirable is it?
- There are obvious benefits from having an Equal Opportunities policy for the employer, employee and community: what are they?
- What mechanisms should Harwoods have in place to ensure no-one is disadvantaged? Some organisations have set up systems to check everyone is treated fairly and equally when applying for jobs, promotion, training, and welfare during working hours.
- What systems seem sensible?

Case 19

> To : Gill Goldman
> From: Molly Weston, Office Manager
> Date : 4.2.9–
> Subject : Attached memo
>
> A complaint from Ashrah Singh is attached herewith. Will you observe that Mr Singh is very annoyed and accuses other staff of victimising him. I thought the matter should be brought to your attention. Do you think we will need to refer to the Race Relation Act re Harassment?
>
> I think it might be a good idea to have a chat with Kevin, Darren and Ted, although I don't think we can single Kevin out for a formal warning as there is no proof he slashed Ashraf's tyres.

To: Molly Weston
From: Ashraf Singh
Date: 31.1.9—
Subject: Vandalism

As I have mentioned to you before, Kevin, Darren and Ted Cox are constantly making abusive remarks to me. Yesterday things went further and someone slashed the tyres of my car whilst it was in the car park. I suspect Kevin, but can't prove it.

I now want the company to issue a formal warning to Kevin and to give informal warnings to Darren and Ted.

If something isn't done to stop this racial harassment I shall take matters up with the Union.

If there is any problem getting my insurers to pay for new tyres, I expect the company to pay.

Issues raised

As a company you have moral as well as legal obligations to all your staff. You must act to prevent racist attacks. How will you proceed in this case? Can you warn Kevin without ascertaining the validity of the accusation?

What would the warning warn him about? Possible sacking? Moving him to a different department? Would some sort of inquiry, with union participation, be useful? Do you think the union would recommend disciplinary proceedings?

Long-term planning resulting from this may be to draw up an Equal Opportunities Statement and publicise it on relevant documentation.

How likely is it that Ashraf Singh is unfairly blaming Kevin for slashing the tyres? Perhaps it was not Kevin. Therefore, perhaps security arrangements in the staff car park need to be improved?

Case 20

Date: 19.3.9–

FAAIU

Dear Gill Goldman

We have recently decided to take up the case of John Gregory, a worker in the delivery room. John has been with Harwoods for seven years and has completed two sets of professional exams to enable him to move up to supervisor, and then into management. However, he has repeatedly been passed over for promotion.

People without John's ability and dedication, experience, or qualifications have meanwhile been promoted. We think John is being discriminated against on the grounds of his homosexuality.

The FAAIU respects the rights of all individuals, whatever their sexual inclination. We want an investigation into why John has not been allowed to achieve all he is capable of.

We request a meeting to discuss the matter further.

Yours sincerely

Thomas Spriggs.

Thomas Spriggs
Regional Branch Officer, FAAIU

Issues raised

What sort of problems do you think homosexual men and women face at work? Do you think it is likely that John has failed to achieve promotion because he is gay? To help decide, John's file should be read. Does he have a case? Has he attended pay review boards? Who has been responsible for adjudicating these? Are his qualifications as good as the Union claims? If he has a case what should be done? What reasons, other than John's homosexuality, might have hindered his progress?

As John is homosexual, the company may think he is HIV positive. Do you think this is a reasonable worry? Some staff may also think that John puts them at risk. What is the company's responsibility to educate their workforce about HIV and AIDS?

Do you think the problems faced by lesbians might be worse than those faced by gay men, or about the same?

What sort of moral obligations do companies have to gay employees? Are any of these obligations enshrined in law?

Case 21

To: Gill Goldman
From: Personnel
Date: 20.6.9–

Following last month's meeting about clarifying our position with respect to Equal Opportunities, we want to place the following ad in 'The Evening Post'. Do you think it makes our equal opportunities policy clear enough? We will use similar copy for all future ads, so please make any changes you feel are necessary.

Food Scientist
Harwoods Soft Drinks, a leading player in the growing soft drinks market, needs to recruit a high-flying food scientist for its rapidly expanding Research and Development department. With responsibility for project management within the carbonated drinks section, the post will require dedication, flair and an uncompromising commitment to quality. Candidates must have at least 5 years industrial experience and a proven track record.

Highly competitive pay and conditions. CV and letters of application to: Personnel Department, Harwoods Soft Drinks, Harwood House, Milestone Road, Rolfham, MR17 8GH.

Harwoods is an Equal Opportunities employer. We welcome applications from all sections of the population, including those traditionally disadvantaged, regardless of sex, colour, creed, religion, ability/disability, age, or sexuality. We actively discourage any discrimination.

Issues raised

What is the point of including an Equal Opportunities statement in job adverts? What do you think of Harwoods' statement? Do you think it would make any difference to the type of candidates who applied?

Is there any point to Equal Opportunities statements unless a company also introduces a monitoring system to monitor the type of people it is employing; what percentage of white males, what percentage of Blacks and Asians, what percentage of women, etc? Monitoring is expensive. Do you think companies should nevertheless introduce monitoring systems? What do you think are the problems of identifying specific ethnic groups?

Do monitoring systems favour only the traditionally disadvantaged or do they create a fairer system for all? Does your college or school operate a monitoring system? As an exercise in monitoring, you might look at the Harwoods organisation chart. What inequalities do you see?

Getting back to the advert, what effect will including an Equal Opportunities statement have on people's perceptions of Harwoods? Do you think the inclusion of an Equal Opportunities statement is just PR, or do you think that is over-cynical?

Below is an example of an Equal Opportunities Monitoring Sheet to help you consider the issue.

Equal Opportunities Monitoring Sheet

This company is committed to giving all job applicants an equal chance of employment. To make sure we do not unintentionally discriminate against anyone, we would be grateful if you would complete the following anonymous form.

POST APPLIED FOR:
SEX:　　MALE/FEMALE　　　　　DATE:
AGE:
DISABILITY:
　Do you have a disability? YES/NO

　Please specify if YES ....

　..

　..

ETHNIC ORIGIN
　Please tick the box that best describes you
Arab　　　　　　　　　　　　　　　　　　☐
Asian　　　　　　　　　　　　　　　　　　☐
Black　　　　　　　　　　　　　　　　　　☐
Chinese　　　　　　　　　　　　　　　　　☐
Hispanic　　　　　　　　　　　　　　　　　☐
White　　　　　　　　　　　　　　　　　　☐
Other　　　　　　　　　　　　　　　　　　☐

Thank you. This form will **not** be used in the selection process.

FOR OFFICE USE ONLY
CANDIDATE WAS: APPOINTED; INTERVIEWED; NOT INTERVIEWED

Case 22

To: Gill Goldman
From: Alec Small, Chief Clerk, Administration
Date: 18.8.9–
Subject: Efficient timekeeping

I note from a recent company newsletter that the company is now concerned with timekeeping. I would therefore like to bring the following to your attention:

1. Women with children in school leave early to pick them up.
2. The Muslims in the factory leave work five times a day to pray at the local mosque.

Surely neither of these should be allowed.

Alec Small

Issues raised

This memo raises an important issue but the tone and attitude of Alec Small does not seem constructive.

In this case the demands of a strictly applied Equal Opportunities policy conflict with the company's need for fairly strict timekeeping.

The needs of working women have been touched on before (Case 7). If women are to combine the dual roles of mother/homemaker and breadwinner, then business is going to have to adapt and allow flexible working hours. Do you think Harwoods might be prepared to be flexible and allow women with school-aged children to start early or work through their lunch hours to make up their hours? Would this cause a lot of disruption?

The case of the Muslims is very difficult. If Muslims leave work five times a day, that creates terrible disruption and would conflict badly with the economic aims of the company. What do you think the company should do? What do you think the Muslims should do? Do you think this case concerns religious intolerance or hard economics? What happens when economics conflicts with Equal Opportunities? What should happen?

Note: Muslims pray five times in 24 hours. Some of the prayers fall outside normal working hours. It must be assumed the canning factory operates 24 hours, with a shift system. Thus each individual Muslim would probably leave once or twice for a short time for prayers in any given shift. Do not assume that all Muslims will keep strict religious observances or that all people with Arabic/Indian names are Muslims.

Case 23

Rolfham College

Leafy Lane
Rolfham

ref. MR/SAW

10.9.9–

Gill Goldman
Harwoods Soft Drinks
Harwood House
Milestone Road
Rolfham

Dear Gill Goldman

I am responsible for arranging work experience placements for students in our Special Needs Unit. Such students may have either moderate learning difficulties or severe learning difficulties.

As part of our strategy to provide all students with experience of the world of work, we ask firms within the community to provide unpaid placements or shadowing opportunities for our Special Needs students.

We have a student, Gary Fox, who has expressed an interest in working for you. He is 21, and wheelchair-bound, having muscular dystrophy. He is intelligent and has good oral communication skills. His writing is poor but he is computer literate and able to use a word processor, and telephone.

The placement would be for three weeks during the Easter period next year. I look forward to an early reply if possible.

Your sincerely

Mo Ramada.

Mo Ramada
Work Experience Coordinator
Special Needs Unit
Rolfham College

Issues raised

Can the company cope with a disabled student? Are there any ramps in the area Gary may be working in? Are other employees likely to know how to react to him? Are there any reasons that Harwoods might prefer to take an able-bodied student? Is this fair?

This would be a good opportunity to provide a service to the local community. Why should Harwoods provide this sort of service to the community? How would their image be affected if they refused to take Gary?

Thinking about your own work placements, what sort of thing do you think the managers at the companies you visit take into account when deciding whether to take you? What are the advantages and disadvantages to companies of taking students on work placements?

In-tray
exercises: 5
Advertising, PR,
marketing

Some of the moral conflicts surrounding advertising, marketing and PR have already been touched on (Cases 20 and 21).

When working through this section, you should think about:

- The way in which you are influenced by advertising and the power of the media. What sort of moral obligation do you think advertisers have? What are their legal obligations? Find out as much as you can about the ASA (Advertising Standards Authority).
- What is the point of advertising, marketing and PR?
- Some advertisements play on our desire to be attractive to others, or on our fears and insecurity, or on our ambitions, even if we don't recognise this when we buy. How far do you think this is defensible?
- What types of promotions tempt you to buy a product? Free gifts, competitions, etc?
- Advertising is needed to keep a company competitive. In theory competition ensures prices are kept down and provides choice for the consumer. Do you think there are any unethical aspects of competition?
- Can advertising reinforce stereotypes? Think of some examples. Is there any connection with the issues you've considered under the Equal Opportunities heading?

Case 24

To: Gill Goldman
From: Sally Browne, Publicity
Date: 1.7.9–
Subject: Publicity Campaign

We are planning the promotion of our new flavour soft drink, a combination of orange, pineapple and strawberry. The name has not yet been decided.

The prime target will be children and young people, so we are considering extensive TV advertising during children's programmes and in comics and teen magazines.

We have a meeting with the advertising agency next week, and in the meantime I would value your ideas on:

a) free badges given with each purchase;
b) tokens given with each purchase to be collected and exchanged for a more valuable gift;
c) whether we could get endorsements for the product on health grounds; a high fruit content, low sugar content, and the fact that it is additive free;
d) getting a children's TV celebrity to endorse the product.

Any other ideas you have would be welcome.

Sally Browne

Issues raised

There is the suggestion that free gifts are given away with the product to improve its desirability. How far is this legitimate? Is it a valid use of natural resources?

How do you feel about the suggestion that the product could be sold on health grounds? Is it significantly different from other similar products on the market? Remember canned soft drinks are not usually well known for their part in a healthy diet, particularly with regard to their sugar/saccharin/caffeine content. See Case 33 from Geoff Smart on the labelling scheme and also Case 14 about dentists' criticism.

Do you think advertisers should target children? Are they a legitimate target or not? If not, why not?

Case 25

To: Gill Goldman
From: Lloyd Smith, Design
Date: 17.8.9–
Subject: Advertising

The enclosed advertisement was recently refused publication in a women's magazine on the grounds of sexism. The decision was surprising, as this advertisement has worked well on hoardings. Could you inform the agency and make it plain to them that they are only to suggest ways of advertising that do not lead us into this sort of situation again.

The decision means that in the short-term we will fail to reach one of our principal target areas, that of the 16–24 single woman, and I am sure that I do not need to impress on you the need for maximising this market. This fact should be impressed on the agency. I think we should hint to them that we are considering using another agency.

Any thoughts?

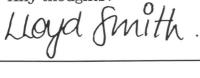

Harwoods...it's the can that gets the man!

Issues raised

What do you consider constitutes a sexist advert? Obviously this one has not broken the law, but has still managed to cause offence. A sexist advertisement could be one which showed no more than a stereotyped picture of women; attractive, sex symbol, available, fickle, flirtatious, unintelligent and subservient to men.

Why do you think the advert worked well on hoardings, but was rejected by a women's magazine? Do you think the company should change its advertising agency? How can Harwoods make sure that future adverts are vetted before being sent out? Would continuing such advertisements bring bad publicity?

Lloyd seems most concerned with the refusal to publish the advert in terms of the loss of a potential market. Do you think this is an appropriate reaction to the problem?

Is there a need to reassert the company's Equal Opportunities Policy, or to write one if necessary?

Case 26

To: Gill Goldman
From: Asad Fareed, Research and Development
Date: 22.7.9–

In one of our publicity handouts we recently claimed that our new banana flavoured drink *Bang!* contained enough potassium to meet the recommended daily amount (RDA) for the average adult. This is, in fact, not true. Although bananas are rich in potassium, which is important to the body's metabolism, our drink does not contain any at all. I think we should pulp all remaining handouts, before someone notices the inaccuracy.

Asad Fareed

Issues raised

Why do you think Harwoods was so keen to claim that *Bang!* contained potassium? Do you think a company would knowingly put out false information?

What are the legal requirements concerning truth in advertisements and PR handouts?

How do you think the marketing department would react to being told its handouts were inaccurate? Would it pulp the handouts?

Do you think Asad Fareed was most concerned about the inaccuracy, or that people outside Harwoods would notice it?

Case 27

To: Gill Goldman
From: Geoff Smart
Date: 24.10.9–

I feel that the *Evening Post* is unduly critical of our operations; think of the recent articles on pollution in local rivers, women returning to work and children's health. All of these were critical of Harwoods.

Can we stop the *Evening Post* printing unflattering stories about us? Are we doing enough to encourage friendly links with local journalists? A lunch or two might not go amiss.

Geoff Smart.

Issues raised

This case is essentially about freedom of the press and the role of PR. Should the press have complete freedom to publish whatever it likes? If not, why not? (Think about the libel laws.)

Specifically on business issues, the press is frequently responsible for uncovering bad practice, irresponsible behaviour and even fraud. List some recent examples. Do you think Gill Goldman should try and 'buy' the *Evening Post*? Do you agree that taking journalists out to lunch might change things?

Case 28

To: Gill Goldman
From: J Edmund Horowitz
Date: 3.10.9–
Subject: Community Involvement

As you know Leisure Products Inc. is committed to recognising its wider responsibility to the local communities in which it works, and to the planet in general. Company policy determines larger scale involvement. In the States this has included a company-wide can recycling policy, office paper collection and recycling, and only investing in socially responsible ways.

However, in terms of the local community, we feel that it is sensible to let the particular communities in which we are involved decide for themselves the ways we could be of benefit to them. Quite obviously we are primarily a profit-making organisation, but are committed also to improving the lives of those living in the communities we serve.

What I would like you to do is to suggest a list of possible ways Leisure Products Inc., and Harwoods PLC in particular, could help the local community in Rolfham. To give you an idea of the sort of thing we are looking for, I have listed similar projects. Recently a factory of ours in Canada built a community centre; our administrative headquarters in New York elected to convert to disabled access much of the local shopping centre, and to start a literacy project; and the Indian sector set up a sponsorship scheme whereby locals unable to fund themselves could continue their education.

Please let me have this in time for the Directors' Meeting next month.

J.E. Horowitz

Issues raised

This memo is from the Chairperson himself. How important is this memo? Why? How would you find out what the workforce/community themselves wanted? Would there be benefits in having groups of workers discussing the issues? Are such groups a good thing? What are their disadvantages? (For the workers, this responsibility may be on top of their usual jobs and may provide a great deal of work with no extra support or pay.)

Do you think Horowitz's ideas are shared by workers throughout the company? Do you think a company might be concerned about its local image for purely cynical reasons, connected with PR, or out of genuine concern for the wellbeing of local people (including, of course, members of its own workforce)?

IN-TRAY EXERCISES: 6 ENVIRONMENTAL ISSUES

The environment is currently a popular issue, but it is a complex one. Your surroundings, local and global, make up the environment.

- The street you live in is your local environment. Environmental concerns here may be litter, dogs, noise, traffic pollution, smoke, smell, effluent or eyesores from local industry, or the policies of local councils on those issues.
- Can you name any specific current environmental issues in your area? What steps are being taken in your local area to safeguard the environment? What more could you do?
- Global issues affect everyone in the world. Your actions may affect people many miles away, and the results may not be immediately apparent, e.g. chemicals produced by factories in industrial areas destroy forests and crops in other countries. Similarly, our western consumer society has created a demand for products which destroy irreplaceable natural resources. The rainforests of South America are very important globally because the trees produce oxygen which is necessary to maintain the ozone layer. Chopping down trees is a quick way to satisfy industry and consumers, but eventually will damage the health and survival of people all round the world.
- What do you use that will damage the ozone layer either in its production or in its use? Any of these?

  – car/motorbike   – paint aerosols
  – hairspray   – goods with a lot of packaging

  Do you know of any alternative products? Do you think that if the packaging says 'environmentally friendly' it is necessarily OK? What steps do you take to help the global environment. What further steps could you take? E.g. do you recycle any of these?

  – glass   – paper
  – plastic   – kitchen waste
  – polythene bags   – water

Case 29

To: Gill Goldman, Management Advisory Team
From: Phil Poole, Chair, Accounts Dept Monthly
      Group Meeting
Date: 14.9.9–
Subject: Office Refurbishments (Plants)

We acknowledge the considerable work that you have done recently in our department, redecorating and generally brightening up the environment. In general we are very impressed with the improvement.

However we were disappointed to see that the plants you had used were Yucca plants.

Yucca plants are often parts of rainforest trees that have been chopped down and dismembered. By purchasing a number of these, as the company obviously has, it has contributed to the destruction of the rainforests. These forests are, as you are aware, essential resources for the whole planet in terms of air replenishment, the discovery of new species and medicines, and furthermore they are essential for the many people who live there.

We would request that in future you order more environmentally friendly products. In the meantime we will try and ensure that our Yuccas survive and thrive as there is no point in getting rid of them.

Phil Poole.

Issues raised

The company needs to examine its supply. Is the issue of rainforest destruction an important one for Harwoods? The environment is obviously an issue for some of the staff, so perhaps the company should take note. Perhaps the company is concerned, but just didn't know about the role of Yuccas.

A working party could be created to examine how the company's actions might affect the environment.

Did you know that the purchase of a Yucca plant might contribute to the destruction of the rainforests? Now that you know this, will you refuse to buy Yuccas on ethical grounds? That is, will you act as an ethical consumer?

Case 30

ref. MT/VW

19.6.9–

Ms G Goldman

Joseph Harwood PLC

Milestone Road

Rolfham

MR17 8GH

Downtown Garages

124–130 Main Street

Rolfham

Telephone 0987 77544

Dear Gill Goldman

Greening company cars

We are inviting all business clients to join us in a special clean up operation for the nineties.

The public are becoming more environmentally conscious, and companies with a green image have noticed significant support and an increased market share as a result of this trend. It makes sense to help the environment, and at the same time to help your own profitability. So consider carrying out these simple, inexpensive adaptations or replacing your current vehicles during our special offer for those who are serious about pollution control.

For one month only we offer **either**:

1. conversion of engines to use lead free petrol FREE OF CHARGE
or
2. installation of CAD systems AT LESS THAN HALF PRICE in all company vehicles under two years old.
   This efficient system cleans ALL emissions from the car, ensuring totally pollution-free driving. Normal cost of the system and installation £250.00, BUT for the next month our price is only £100.
or
3. special discounts on new fleet vehicles with anti-pollution features.
   Choose from VW, Vauxhall, or Ford models which incorporate the above features as standard. Substantial discounts are available to organisations buying or leasing fleet vehicles. For further details on this offer contact Kath Higgins on ext. 24.

Yours sincerely

Michael Thomas

Michael Thomas

Managing Director

Issues raised

Are cars, even cars with catalytic converters using unleaded petrol, environmentally friendly? Should the provision of company cars be encouraged? Is the introduction of unleaded petrol a major environmental step? The benzine which replaces the lubricating lead is possibly carcinogenic. If there was genuine concern and financial commitment to environmental concerns the more expensive catalytic converters would be fitted where possible. Is this something Harwoods should do?

Even if the management are relatively unconcerned about the environment, do you think they should make sure company cars have catalytic converters as a PR exercise?

Case 31

To: Gill Goldman
From: Julian Costello
Date: 21.10.9–

I have discussed with Sally Browne the new soft drink to be launched in the summer. She is keen that it should look quite special and different, so I wondered about packaging it in waxed paper cartons instead of traditional cans.

What do you think? Are there implications in terms of raw materials? Recycling? Litter? Let me have your comments.

Julian Costello.

Issues raised

Waxed paper is less environmentally friendly than reusable materials, such as aluminium, or even glass. Paper is made from wood. Do you think trees should be destroyed to satisfy consumer demand for a non-essential product like a soft drink?

Recycling paper is not necessarily an environmentally friendly process. Why not? See if you can find out about the recycling process.

Do you drop litter? Why do you think people drop litter? In what ways does litter influence an environment?

Would you recommend packaging the drinks in waxed paper or not? How much is this a moral decision and how much one concerned with economics and/or image and marketing? How much should it be an ethical decision?

Case 32

To: Gill Goldman
From: Sally Browne
Date: 7.7.9–

I saw this in *The Reporter* last night. Any comment?

Do you think that we should write and tell her that we are considering waxed cartons? Perhaps we should contact the paper and let them know we're considering cartons. We could invite Ms Gordon to visit the factory and invite someone from *The Evening Post*. The paper would then run the story and we'd get some good publicity. They might even include a photo!

Sally Browne

Letter to the Editor

I am disgusted at the amount of litter in our town. The youth of today leave drinks cans lying in the street, even when disposal bins are provided nearby.

While in no way sympathising with these litter louts, I do think the manufacturers of soft drinks should package them in waxed cartons instead of metal cans. Paper cartons would be easier to dispose of, and easier to carry home when empty.

Surely, our local drinks factory should be looking into this possibility?

Ms G Gordon, Rolfham.

Issues raised

As a local employer and manufacturer of soft drinks you could respond to the letter as a public relations exercise as Sally Browne seems to suggest. Do you think this is an appropriate response?

Whatever packaging it decides upon, do you think there would be a case for suggesting that Harwoods set up a recycling centre in Rolfham, providing recycling bins for glass, aluminium and paper. Perhaps you could prepare such a proposal to the Board.

Case 33

To: Gill Goldman
From: Geoff Smart, Marketing
Date: 11.8.9–
Subject: Environmentally friendly labelling schemes

I have recently been researching the German scheme for endorsing environmentally friendly products, as a similar scheme is soon to be introduced here and we need to know the implications for our products. The German label is called the Blue Angel, and for more than a decade has been awarded to companies whose products are considered to be genuinely environmentally friendly.

Obviously such an endorsement has marketing advantages, and I recommend that Harwoods look carefully into eligibility for such a label when similar schemes are introduced here in Britain. However, I should point out that to qualify the product must not only be 'green' in content and disposability, but the whole manufacturing process and policy of the producer must be equally environmentally sound.

This means we would need to check on:
1. How 'green' our drinks are.
2. Harwoods' sources of raw materials, to ensure that they do not come from countries which exploit the planet and the workers.
3. The manufacturing process and waste disposal. Is every effort being made to reduce pollution in all areas of production? Do we have any system for monitoring waste products for the factory?
4. The company's responsibilities towards its workers.
5. Whether our advertising and marketing are ethically sound.

With the European single market this will become an important issue, so I should be grateful if you would provide an outline

Issues raised

Rather than jumping on the bandwagon in terms of environmentally friendly products, the company should investigate the labelling scheme; the products would have to be genuinely kind to the environment not only in terms of content and disposability but also in terms of the manufacturing process. Would Harwoods qualify? Labelling will probably receive higher priority as moving further into Europe will disadvantage the company unless it is able to compete.

Does such a labelling scheme really ensure genuine responsibility towards the environment? Or is it only a marketing strategy?

See Case 36 (new musquat drink) and Case 31 (packaging).

In-tray exercises: 7
Human rights

When working through this section, you should think about the points below.

- Do all human beings have access to the same rights?
- Think about what we consider to be our rights: justice, freedom of speech, religion, freedom from persecution, health care, education, food, employment, fair pay for work.
- Can you add others?

  Do all people in this country enjoy these rights?

  Do people in other countries have them? If not, why not?

  What do you think our responsibility is towards these people?

  What do you think Harwoods' responsibility is towards them?
- Because many third world countries would like to have overseas organisations investing in them, in order to gain access to foreign currency, they may be unlikely to cause a fuss about working conditions and rates of pay. Given this situation, any investing multinational is in a very powerful position and, seeing the opportunity for a high profit, may disregard the rights of those it employs.

Case 34

To: Gill Goldman
From: Geoff Smart
Date: 20.12.9–
Subject: Article in the newspaper

I noticed this article in yesterday's edition of *The Evening Post* and thought you would be interested, and horrified, to know what criticisms are being made about us. The writer investigates the activities of various multinational firms like ours; the part which particularly concerns us is attached.

Geoff Smart.

Workers in Mexico and South America are exploited in two ways. They are forced to accept low wages as they have no rights or power to negotiate. In one case a well-known soft drinks manufacturer is paying factory workers only 10 per cent of the wages it pays its British employees. Even lower are the wages this same company pays the casual labourers who pick fruit. Their weekly wage has the equivalent buying power of £3 per week in Britain, well below the poverty line.

Secondly, advantage is also taken of the fact that the countries in which this multinational company operates have few, if any, safety laws. This means that workplace safety levels can be ignored. Practices which would be illegal here are accepted as the norm there. No checks on machine safety, exposure to harmful substances, or aspects of working conditions like heat, light and ventilation are required. Therefore the great profit-makers are keen to extend their empire in countries like these where overheads are so low.

Large savings can be made if the workers are paid less and subjected to higher risks of personal injury than in the expensive factories of Britain. Their products should carry the warning label 'Profits cost lives'.

Issues raised

Clearly the writer of this newspaper article is giving a biased view of the operations of multinational organisations, implying that all such companies exploit their workers in Third World countries. However, there are some serious issues here to think about.

- What is a fair wage to pay workers doing the same jobs in different countries with different economic circumstances, needs and expectations? Is the company exploiting its workers in Third World countries by paying them less than those in Britain?

- What is likely to be the effect of paying higher wages than are generally paid elsewhere in the poorer country?
- With regard to safety, think of the industrial accident at Bhopal where many people died or were maimed for life. The safety standards allowed in operation there would not have been legal in this country.
- Why would some companies neglect both the safety of their workers and that of the community near the factory?
- Why would some companies choose to maintain rigorous safety standards comparable with those operating in Britain?
- Is a company under any obligation to do more than meet the bare legal requirements?

Case 35

To: Gill Goldman
From: Geoff Smart, Marketing Department
Date: 17.1.9–

I feel that we are getting a lot of bad publicity from our African operation. Someone from Radio 4 has phoned us up to ask us to appear on a programme called 'Marketing in the Third World', dealing with selling apparently unnecessary products to the developing world.

You may remember powdered milk companies have recently received poor publicity as a result of similar reports, and I am therefore concerned.

The programme wishes to discuss why we market our canned soft drinks with such heavy advertising. It claims that they are unhealthy for children and young adults because of their high sugar content, and that they are too expensive. Could you prepare a briefing sheet listing the pros and cons of working in such a market? Could we improve the situation? What do our competitors do?

Do we have any community action schemes designed to help our customers in developing countries?

Geoff Smart.

Issues raised

Does the company need to sell to the Third World? Will it do more harm than good? How can you legitimately answer criticism of unhealthy, expensive and relatively unimportant products being pushed in the Third World? Is this exploitation? Do you think Leisure Products Inc. will continue to support such a move, given its desire to be more socially responsible? What would the loss of sales in developing countries do to the company's profits?

What might the company need to do to counterbalance the loss of markets in the developing world? Should it decide no longer to sell to them?

This is a useful example of the impact of the media on environmental awareness. List some cases where you have learned through the media, of businesses exploiting the Third World.

Case 36

To: Gill Goldman
From: Asad Fareed, Research and Development
     Division Head
Date: 28.2.9–
Subject: Report on supplies of tropical fruit

Introduction

Following discussions of the Production, Research and Marketing divisions about the possibility of producing a new soft drink based on the tropical fruit musquat, I have undertaken research into this proposal. Sources of supply were investigated by reference to existing suppliers, contacts in the World Fruit Growers Federation, and by visits to prospective growing sites.

Information

Musquat culture
Musquats grow only in tropical conditions, and are currently produced and exported in commercial quantities from very few countries.

Current sources
Harwoods currently buy only small quantities of musquats; 4 per cent of all fruit purchased. This comes from the Middle East, and is priced at 10 per cent above the world average price for musquats. This contract is due for review/renewal next year.

Alternative sources
A large established grower in West Africa produces high quality fruit, comparable with that which Harwoods currently obtains from the Middle East, at 2 per cent over average world prices. Transportation costs are extra. This grower supplies Harwoods' main competitors in Europe.

New musquat plantations are being started in West Africa, 200 miles nearer to the coast than the existing ones. They are being created on virgin land, recently cleared of forest, and are planned to be extensive. The cost is estimated to be 3 per cent below the average world price, and transportation costs will be less because of improved proximity to the port.

In South America many acres of forest are about to be felled to make way for cultivation of cash crops, including coffee and musquats. Experts consider these sites to be ideal for musquat production, and estimate prices at least 7 per cent below current average world prices.

Conclusions

It would appear unwise to renew the contract with Harwoods' current supplier for the following reasons:

- other sources are currently significantly cheaper;
- our demands will be very much increased over present levels if the new drink is launched. Therefore the savings on fruit from either of the other two sources will be significantly greater;
- to purchase fruit from the same grower as our competitors will reduce our control of the market;
- therefore, it is recommended that Harwoods negotiate a purchasing contract with a new supplier, either in West Africa or South America.

Asad Fareed

Issues raised

The issue here is whether Harwoods should consider the effects of its actions upon the world environment and Third World communities.

If Harwoods chooses to buy fruit from countries where forests have been destroyed to create space to grow these cash crops, to what extent is it responsible for destroying that forest and/or the ozone layer? Should it pay more for its fruit to avoid contributing to the destruction of the rainforest?

What is the nature of the conflict between Harwoods' responsibility to its shareholders and to the environment?

What is the effect upon the people who live in the forest areas? Do they benefit by earning better wages, or do they lose out by growing a crop they cannot use themselves?

What would be the long-term effects on communities where such cash crops became the mainstay of the economy? What might the implications be for social organisation and stability? For culture? For political development?

Think about how this case concerns both the protection of the environment and the respect for human rights.

RESOURCES

To provide a useful resource bank it is essential that the material it contains is topical and up-to-date. Therefore, we suggest below some sources of information on the range of issues raised in the case-study. They include books and publications which regularly or occasionally cover items of interest, and organisations whose activities relate to the topic.

Adams, R. (ed), *Antarctica: Voices from the Silent Continent* Hodder & Stoughton 1990

Business in Society: a new initiative building on what leaders in management predict for tomorrow New Initiatives Ltd (071 435 5000)

Business Network
18 Well Walk
London
NW3 1LD

Cowell, A. *Decade of Destruction* Hodder & Stoughton 1990

Croner's
Employment Law
Croner's Health and Safety at Work
Croner Publications Ltd
Croner House
London Road
Kingston upon Thames
KT2 6SR

Daunce, G. *After the Crash: the emergence of the Rainbow Economy* Green Print 1988

Ecologist
Corner House
Station Road
Sturminster Newton
Dorset
DT10 1BB

Ecology Building Society
18 Station Road
Cross Hills
Keighley
BD20 7EH
Who produce a video *Invest in the Alternative*

Elkington, J. *A Year in the Greenhouse; an environmental diary* Gollancz

Elkington J. and J. Hailes *The Green Consumer's Supermarket Shopping Guide* Gollancz

Ethical Consumer
ECRA Publishing Ltd
100 Gretney Walk
Moss Side
Manchester
M15 5ND
Published bi-monthly

Friends of the Earth
26–28 Underwood Street
London
N1 7JQ

Independent Guide to Ethical Pension Funds

Independent Guide to Socially Responsible Investment Funds

Labour Research Department leaflets on related topics
Labour Research Department Publications
78 Blackfriars Road
London
SE1 8HF

Which Magazine
Consumers Association